SAGE LINE 50 V12

Covers Accountant, Accountant Plus and Financial Controller

GILLIAN GILERT

In easy steps is an imprint of Computer Step
Southfield Road · Southam
Warwickshire CV47 0FB · United Kingdom
www.ineasysteps.com

Notice of Liability
Every effort has been made to ensure that this book contains accurate and
current information. However, Computer Step and the author shall not be
liable for any loss or damage suffered by readers as a result of any information
contained herein.

Trademarks
Sage Line 50®, Accountant®, Accountant Plus® and Financial Controller® are
all registered trademarks of The Sage Group Plc. Microsoft® and Windows®
are registered trademarks of Microsoft Corporation. All other trademarks are
acknowledged as belonging to their respective companies.

Printed and bound in the United Kingdom

ISBN 13 978-1-84078-310-0
ISBN 10 1-84078-310-9

Table of Contents

The Bank 57

Products 73

Invoices 87

Opening Balances

13

Data Management

14

The Task Manager

15

Index

Getting Started

This chapter takes you through the stages of preparing Sage Line 50 for use. It explains initial procedures for setting up the various defaults required by the program.

Covers

Chapter One

Introduction

All businesses need to keep accurate records of their accounts, but even with a computer program, if the information is not entered correctly, then the accounts could still be wrong. After all, it's easy to blame the computer!

Working through Sage Line 50 V12 in easy steps

This book explains in simple, easy stages how to perform the main tasks required for keeping computerised business accounts. The following chapters show how to:

Make use of the demo data provided with Sage Line 50 to fully familiarise yourself with the program before getting started. To do this simply click File, Open from the main menu and select Open Demo Data.

- Set defaults and Company preferences.

- Create customer & supplier records and set up price lists.

- Set up opening balances, maintain Bank accounts.

- Maintain the Nominal Ledger and run an audit trail.

- Generate sales orders and control stock.

- Print invoices, credit notes and statements.

- Produce history and financial reports.

'Preparing to start' checklist

Before getting started with Sage Line 50, work through the checklist below.

Some things, once entered, cannot be easily changed. Therefore, make sure you have all the relevant information to hand before using Sage Line 50 for the first time.

- Check the start date of your company's financial year.

- Check with an accountant which VAT scheme is used.

- Draw up a list of defaults to use.

- Decide on users and passwords.

- Backup the data if updating Sage.

- Have customer, supplier and bank details to hand.

- Product details, recommend a stock take.

With Sage Line 50 V12 it is possible to change the Financial Year start date after you have already commenced using the program.

- A list of all opening balances.

Note: the program folder is now called Sage Accounts, not Line 50.

Starting Sage Line 50

Alternatively, if a shortcut has been set up on the Windows desktop, you can open Sage Line 50 by double-clicking on the shortcut icon:

Turn on your computer and wait for the Windows Desktop to appear. To start Sage Line 50 do the following:

1 Click on Start

2 Point to Programs – a selection appears

Remember that your reporting will not be accurate until all your opening balances have been entered. Ask your accountant for these, if possible before you start using Line 50.

3 Point to Sage Accounts folder

4 Click on Sage Accounts

5 The Sage Line 50 desktop appears

With Sage Line 50 you can create multiple delivery addresses so that you can have goods delivered to a number of customer sites whilst specifying a different invoice address.

Sage Line 50 Desktop Views

New in Line 50 v12, the View selector lets you change the display in the Sage desktop work area. Although the options vary from module to module, typically the views may include a List display, a Process Map and a Dashboard.

For instant help in any Sage window, simply press the F1 help key.

A Process Map (Customer) is shown on Page 9, whilst the Nominal Ledger List view is shown below. To switch views, simply do the following:

2 Select Company Dashboard

1 Click on Change View

The Process Map shows the workflow associated with the selected group and is a quick and convenient way of switching between related modules.

2 The Company Dashboard shows important trading information about your business. Click here to print

Regularly use the Dashboard views to keep track of how your business is progressing. For example, you can quickly view your aged debtors or creditors without having to run separate reports, see which are your top customers or which stock is running low.

Settings

Before Sage Line 50 can be used there are a number of settings and defaults that need to be entered. The rest of this chapter shows how to do this. When required, select the appropriate settings option from the following list:

Click Help on the Sage Line 50 menu bar, then Shortcut Keys, to bring up a diagram of the available shortcuts. Click on the diagram to close it.

Click on Settings on the Menu bar

2 Click on the option required

Using Passwords

The Data Protection Act requires that any system containing confidential information, i.e., financial details etc., should be protected against unauthorised access. Sage Line 50 uses a password to achieve this. Once you set a password, Sage Line 50 always prompts you for it at startup.

As with any password, you should avoid writing it down if at all possible. Therefore, try to choose a password that is both easy for you to remember but difficult for someone else to discover. You can decrease the chance of somebody accidentally finding out your password by using a mixture of letters and numbers instead of an actual word.

Try to avoid using obvious things like a name, phone number or car registration as a password. These are far too easy to guess.

From the Settings menu click on Change Password

2 Type your password here

3 Repeat the password here for confirmation

4 Click OK to save password

Company Preferences

When you run Sage Line 50 for the first time the Easy Startup Wizard asked for your Company details. Alternatively, after selecting Company Preferences from the settings options, you can enter these details as follows:

Use the Tab key instead of your mouse to move onto the next line or box.

1 Enter your company name here

2 Enter your full address details in this box

3 E-Mail and Web addresses go here

4 Enter VAT & Credit Ref No's if appropriate

5 Click OK to finish

You can enter an alternative address for deliveries by clicking on the Delivery Addresses button.

Departments, Products and Fixed Assets Categories

After selecting Configuration from the settings options, you can assign transactions to different departments and divide products and fixed assets into different categories for analysis:

To have Sage Line 50 print your company details on your stationery, select the Reporting tab and tick the Print Address on Stationery box in the Printing section.

1 Select tab & click on the first blank entry

2 Click Edit & enter name

3 Click OK

4 Click Apply button to use

5 Repeat steps 1–4 for Products & Fixed Assets

Setting up & checking Tax Codes

Sage Line 50 already has the standard UK and EC VAT Rates set for you together with the code T1 (standard rate – currently 17.5%) set as the default tax code. Here is a list of the codes automatically set up during installation:

It is important to use the correct VAT codes. If unsure of current UK or EU VAT Tax rates then contact HM Revenue & Customs.

T0	–	zero rated transactions
T1	–	standard rate
T2	–	exempt transactions
T4	–	sales to customers in EC★
T7	–	zero rated purchases from suppliers in EC★
T8	–	standard rated purchases from suppliers in EC★

T1 is the standard UK VAT rate code.

T9	–	transactions not involving VAT

(★ Outside the UK)

There are 100 VAT codes available in Sage Line 50. To enter or change VAT tax rates, use Configuration from the settings options:

1 Click Tax Codes tab & required code

2 Click Edit

Sage Line 50 uses T9 as the default tax code for all the routines that are non-vatable, e.g. journal entries error corrections and Bank.

3 Enter percentage rate

4 Tick if VAT rate is for an EC Code

6 Click Apply to use

5 Enter Description & click OK

Financial Year

The start of the financial year is entered during the installation of Sage Line 50 or before entering any transactions, but it is now possible to change it:

1 From Settings on the menu bar click on Financial Year

2 To change year select the Change button

3 Click Yes in the next two prompt windows, select year & click OK

Account Status

A handy feature within Line 50 is that you can assign an account status to each of your accounts. You can add an account status at any time to the ten already set up via the Configuration Editor:

1 Click on Account Status tab then highlight a blank line

2 Click Edit

3 Enter Status Name here

4 Click here if you want this status to place accounts 'on hold'

6 Click Apply to use

5 Click OK

Currency & the Euro

Sage Line 50 is already set up with the currencies of the EC countries, but not the exchange rates. These details can be edited or other countries set up as required:

Simply press F5 to access the Euro Calculator in any numeric field that displays a calculator button.

1 Click on Settings, Currencies and highlight the currency you want to edit or select the first blank record to enter a new currency

The calculator can be used to either view an amount converted from Sterling to a Euro/Foreign Currency or to convert a Euro/Foreign Currency amount to Sterling.

2 Click Edit to bring up the Edit Currency box

4 The Currency symbol is entered here

3 Enter the name of the Currency

5 The Currency Code goes here

Exchange rates change frequently, so make sure you have the latest rates entered before recording a foreign currency transaction. Up to date rates are available from a number of sources, including the Internet (e.g. www.xe.com).

6 Enter the Currency exchange rate

7 The reverse exchange rate appears here

8 Enter the Major and Minor currency units

9 Click OK, then Close the Currencies box

Customer & Supplier Defaults

When creating a new customer or supplier, details about credit limit, terms, discount etc. are needed. Customer and Supplier records are discussed in Chapters Two & Three respectively but before this, defaults need to be set up.

For customers, default nominal codes (N/C) start at 4000.

1 Select Customer Defaults from the Settings options

2 Select this Tab to enter the defaults for your customer records

A customer can be a member of a price list. However, as a customer can only belong to one price list, if you want to change the list that the selected customer belongs to, select the price list you require from the drop-down list. Note that on each price list, additional discounts can still be applied.

3 Click on the relevant Tabs to enter Statements, Ageing Balance and Discount defaults

4 Click OK to save Customer Defaults

5 Select Supplier Defaults from the Settings options

6 Enter relevant Supplier Defaults here

Default nominal codes for suppliers start at 5000.

7 Select this Tab to enter Aged Balances Period, specifying calendar months or days

8 Click OK to save Supplier Defaults

Product Defaults

Defaults also need to be set up for Products:

1 Select Product Defaults from the Settings options

Use the Finder button on the right of the Nominal Code box to speed up code entry.

2 Enter the Nominal account code here

3 Allocate the correct Tax Code for the Product

4 Complete the rest of the defaults as necessary

6 Click OK to save this information

5 Enter the Decimal Point placing for the product

Control Accounts

Sage Line 50 uses Control Accounts to make automatic double-entry postings to the ledger.

Unless you have created your own Chart of Accounts, the Control accounts should never need changing.

1 To view or edit these Nominal Codes select Control Accounts from the Settings options

2 To change a Control account click on the nominal code and type the new code or use the Finder button

3 Click OK to save and close or Cancel to abandon changes

Control Account	N/C
Debtors Control	1100
Creditors Control	2100
Default Bank	1200
VAT on Sales	2200
VAT on Purchases	2201
Sales Discount	4009
Purchase Discount	5009
Retained Earnings	3200
Default Sales	4000
Accruals	2109
Prepayments	1103
Bad Debts	8100
Mispostings	9999
Suspense	9998

Finance Rates

Finance rates need to be set up before any credit charges can be applied to your customers.

When a Finance Charge Rate is applied to a transaction, the first rate charged will be applied monthly until the invoice is paid.

1 Select Configuration from the Settings menu and click on the Terms tab to bring up the Finance Charge Rates box

2 Click on Add to enter a new finance rate charge

You must first have set up your finance rates and the date from which they are to be applied before you can use the Charges option on the Customer toolbar.

3 Enter the date the charge is to be applied from

4 Enter the Base Rate as a percentage here

5 Enter an additional charge here if applicable

Use the Delete button on the Finance Charge Rates window to remove any unwanted charges.

6 Click OK to save new finance rate or Cancel to return to the Finance Charge Rates box

7 Click Close to finish

The Customer Ledger

In this chapter you will learn how to use the Customer (Sales) Ledger to maintain customer records and create new ones as well as enter credit notes and invoices. You will also be shown how to view transaction activity and set up a customer price list, as well as produce an overdue payments letter, and you will learn how to apply credit charges and to mark an invoice as disputed.

Covers

Chapter Two

The Importance of Keeping a Financial System

It is essential for all businesses to have a system to record and monitor their business and financial transactions. This information needs to be accurately recorded and kept up to date if it is to present a true financial position.

Regularly monitor your Customer credit using the Manage Credit Control option in the Customer Tasks list. Here you can quickly produce a handy printout of Overdue and Outstanding Debtors useful for chasing payment.

Such a system will involve the recording of transactions using the traditional method of bookkeeping or advanced accounting procedures, where financial reports (i.e. profit & loss statements and balance sheet, etc.) can be produced.

These reports provide the Management with information on sales, purchases, turnover, expenses, debtors and creditors, assets and liabilities, and more importantly, if the business has made a profit.

The Inland Revenue and HM Customs & Excise (if VAT registered), now collectively called HM Revenue and Customs, will also need accurate accounts, which must conform to general bookkeeping and accounting procedures.

This information is also of importance to your Bank Manager, especially if there is a need to borrow money to ease cash flow problems or help set up a new business venture. Likewise, potential investors in your business may first want to see the true financial position of your accounts before making a decision.

Computerised systems have now removed the majority of time consuming and repetitive tasks of manual accounting. Businesses can check their financial status on a daily basis, or over a designated period of time. This valuable information will aid important decision making and business planning and is crucial for forecasting whether a business will succeed or fail.

Sage Line 50 makes keeping computerised accounts easy. Many of the report templates needed are provided with the package, so producing accurate business reports is a simple matter, provided, of course, that all information has been entered correctly. The following chapters guide you through the processes involved in keeping accurate and up to date computerised financial accounts for your business.

The Customers Toolbar

The Customers toolbar provides features for creating customer records and viewing transaction activity, producing invoices and credit notes, marking invoices as disputed and applying credit charges. Customer Statements are produced here, plus letters, a range of reports and generating price lists.

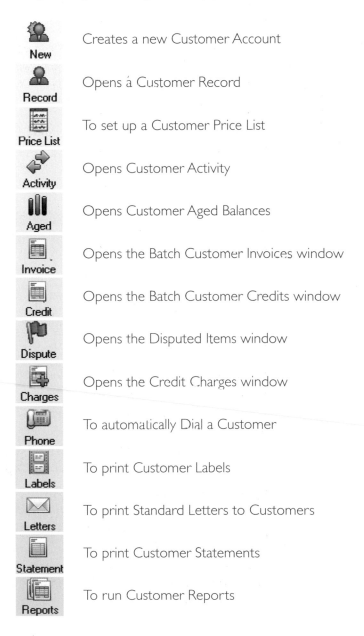

New — Creates a new Customer Account

Record — Opens a Customer Record

Price List — To set up a Customer Price List

Activity — Opens Customer Activity

Aged — Opens Customer Aged Balances

Invoice — Opens the Batch Customer Invoices window

Credit — Opens the Batch Customer Credits window

Dispute — Opens the Disputed Items window

Charges — Opens the Credit Charges window

Phone — To automatically Dial a Customer

Labels — To print Customer Labels

Letters — To print Standard Letters to Customers

Statement — To print Customer Statements

Reports — To run Customer Reports

Creating Customer Records

Within this window, a customer record can be added, edited or deleted. You can also record agreed credit terms and even log any contact you have with a customer, such as telephone calls and who you spoke to.

Use the New wizard for simple step by step instructions for entering a basic new customer record.

1 Select Customers from the Line 50 V12 navigation bar

2 Click on Record to bring up the Customer Record window

Before you can enter an Opening Balance you have to first save the new customer details record.

3 Use Details to store customer name, address and contact information

4 Use the O/B button to enter an Opening Balance where required

The method of entering opening balances is different for Standard VAT and VAT Cash Accounting. Use F1 help key to check.

5 Use the Credit Control tab to enter credit terms for the customer

6 Select Account Status from this drop down box

7 Click Save to store the Customer Record

8 Enter a new record or click Close to finish

Note that the following codes indicate the transaction type:

SI = Sales Invoice
SR = Sales Receipt
SC = Sales Credit Note
SD = Sales Discount
SA = Sales Receipt on Account

Viewing transactions

Once customer activity has taken place, Sage Line 50 offers you a variety of options for checking customer transaction details:

- View customer invoices, receipts, credit notes and balances on a monthly basis, as a graph or table.

- Use the Activity option to see a breakdown of each customer's transactions.

- View or print the Customer's aged balances.

1 Click on the Activity tab in the Customer Record window

Use the Orders tab to quickly view a history of the sales orders a customer has placed with you. Double click on an order in the list to bring up the sales order record.

Use the Tidy List button to clear all transaction sub-items from view.

2 Click here on a transaction to show all items

3 Click on the arrows to scroll through all the transactions

4 Click on Range to select another date range or range of transactions, then click OK

5 Select Close to return to Customer window

Price List

In Sage Line 50 v12, different price lists can be set up and customers allocated to the price list of your choice. For each Price List products can be added and different prices set up accordingly. For example, you can create custom lists for Trade, Retail, Summer or Winter Sales and Special Offers.

To create a new Price List do the following:

Where a selected customer is already on another price list, Line 50 asks if you want to transfer this customer to the new list. Click Yes to transfer the customer to the new list or Yes to All to transfer all customers already on another list to the new list.

1 From the Customers toolbar click on the Price List button to bring up the Price Lists box

2 Click New to open the New Price List window

3 Enter Reference and Name here

4 Click Save

5 Select Customers & click Add to bring up the Add Customers Box

To add more than one customer at a time to your list, simply hold down the Control key and click on your selection during Step 6.

6 Select Customer

7 Click OK

8 Click Save, then Close and Close again to return to the Customers window

Batch Customer Invoice

Where you only know the gross value of an invoice, enter it in the Net box and use the Calc. Net button (or press the F9 shortcut key) to let Line 50 work out the correct Net value and VAT due.

Invoices are important business transaction documents and record detailed information about the goods or services supplied to the customer. Briefly, these details include the invoice number, name and address of the customer, date of sale, details of goods and or services supplied, details of discount, total amount of money due and terms of trade.

There are different types of invoices for the task you are carrying out and Chapter Seven shows you how to create a product or a service invoice, as well as automatically creating an invoice from a sales order. However, any invoices produced manually (Batch Invoices) and sent to customers also need recording. No printout is produced.

To record a batch customer invoice do the following:

1 Choose Invoice from the Customers toolbar

2 Enter the customer Account Code or use the finder button to display a list of codes

3 Change invoice date if different from current system date

For a list of useful data entry Shortcut Keys consult the Handy Reference at the start of this book.

4 Enter the Invoice Number here, and a Ref. Number, as required

5 Change Nominal Code or Department if different from defaults

Always check that the correct Tax Code is used. See page 13.

6 Click Save to update the nominal ledger and customer details (details posted), then Close

7 Enter Net value of invoice here

Batch Customer Credit Note

To check the credit note has been posted, make a note of the balance for the appropriate customer in the Customers window before entering the credit note, then check that the balance has reduced by the correct amount after performing Step 6.

A credit note is used, for example, where an error is made and a customer has been overcharged on an invoice. Sometimes, damaged goods are returned and so a credit note is issued showing the amount due to the customer.

Like batch invoicing, credit notes processed manually need to be entered. To record batch credit notes:

1 Click Credit from the Customers toolbar to bring up the Batch Customer Credits window

2 Enter the customer Account Code

3 The screen displays the defaults for the nominal account code posting, VAT rate to be applied & department

When looking at Customer activity, the transaction type (Tp) code SC indicates a Sales Credit Note.

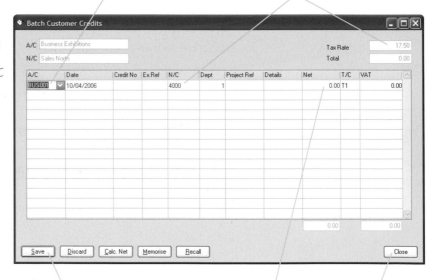

4 Enter credit details for each customer in the same way as for batch invoice

If you need a printout of a credit, generate a product or service credit note from Invoicing on the Sage Line 50 navigation bar and the details will be recorded automatically.

5 Check all values are correct & click Save to post the details or Discard to start again

6 Click Close to return to the Customers window

Debtors Analysis

To identify debtors and monitor cashflow, customers' outstanding balances and transactions need to be regularly checked. These transactions are grouped by the age of the debt, either on calendar months or based on a period of days, e.g. 30, 60 and 90 days etc. Debt chasing letters can be issued if required. A business may use this information to calculate interest charges for late payment.

From the Settings menu simply select Customer Defaults, then the Ageing tab to change the age of the debt from calendar months to period of days, or vice versa.

1 From the Customers window select the required customer

2 Click Aged to bring up the Aged Balances Date Defaults box

3 Enter the date to be used for calculating the aged balances

4 To include payments only up to a particular date, enter that date here

6 To see a graph format click the Graph tab

5 Click OK to bring up the Aged Balances window

When you select the required customers in the Customers window, always check that the dates in the Aged Balance Report Date and the Include Payments Up To boxes cover those selected customers.

7 For a transaction breakdown click on Detailed

8 Click Close to return

Credit Charges

A payment which is 30 days overdue is regarded, by default, as late. If you need to change payment terms, do the following:

Use the Memo box to keep notes on a credit agreement negotiated with the selected customer.

1 From the navigation bar choose the Customers button

2 Highlight the appropriate customer or customers, then click the Record button

3 Click on the Credit Control tab to bring up the Credit Control details box

4 Enter new details in Payment Due

To apply charges to customers whose payments are overdue simply click Charges from the Customers window to run the Credit Charges Wizard.

5 Apply account restrictions here if desired, such as placing account on hold or allowing credit to be charged

Before you can use the Wizard, finance rates must have first been set up.

6 Change any of the other terms as required, then click Save

7 Click Close to return to the Customers window, then Close again

Disputed Invoices

Don't forget to first set up Dispute Reasons using the Configuration Editor. This will then give you more accurate reporting when you need to check why an item has been marked as disputed in the future.

There may be times when an invoice is questioned by the customer, so until an agreement is made the invoice can be marked as disputed. This option also applies to any invoices not fully paid. Once the problem is resolved, you can remove the disputed flag (indicator). To mark an invoice as disputed:

1 Click on the Dispute button in the Customers window to bring up the Disputed Items window

2 Enter the Customer Account Code here and press the Tab key

3 Click on the transaction you want to mark as disputed

To remove the Dispute status of an invoice simply highlight it and click the Dispute button again.

4 Click Dispute

5 Select Reason & Click OK

6 Note that transaction is now marked as 'd'

Remember that if you are using Standard VAT, invoices marked as disputed are still included in the VAT Return.

7 Click Save to record the transaction

8 Click Close to return to the Customers window, then Close again

Customer Reports and Modem

Sage Line 50 provides you with a wide range of ready-designed customer reports to suit the majority of needs. To print or view a customer report, do the following:

The arrow on the right of the Customers toolbar lets you access any buttons that do not fit in the toolbar.

1 Click on the Reports button in the Customers window

2 Click here on the appropriate folder

3 Select the report you require from the list

4 Select output, i.e. Preview

5 Click Generate Report to produce report

6 After printing Close each window

Modem

For some features, you need to have a modem fitted in your PC. By default, the F11 key is set up by Line 50 to open the Control Panel so that you can check if your computer has a modem installed, as follows:

If your computer modem & telephone share the same line you can ring a customer using the Phone button from the Customers toolbar, then just pick up your phone to talk to them.

1 Press the F11 key to bring up the Windows Control Panel

2 Double-click on the Phone and Modem icon

3 Click the Modems tab to see if a modem is fitted

To check if your modem is working correctly, click Properties, then select the Diagnostics tab and click on the Query Modem button.

Customer Letters and Labels

Occasionally, you may have a need to send standard information to a customer, such as change of address, or to chase up an overdue payment. All of the necessary information needed for these letters is taken from your records.

A number of the more common standard letters are provided with Sage Line 50, but alternatively there is the option to create new ones. The new letters can be stored for future use.

Remember to select a customer from the list before clicking the Letters button.

1 From the Customers window, select the customer or customers you want to send a letter to

2 Click the Letters button on the Customers toolbar to bring up the Customer Letters list

To send the same letter (e.g. change of address) to all your customers, first deselect all customers using the Clear button in the Customers window before carrying out Steps 2–7.

3 Click on the letter required

4 Ensure Preview is checked

5 Click Generate Report to produce report

To produce labels for all your customers in one go simply click the clear button before pressing the Labels button on the Customers toolbar.

6 If correct, click Print, then OK

7 Click Close

The Customer Statement

To keep customers up to date about their financial position, customer statements should be sent out on a regular basis, normally once a month. The statement shows details of all recorded customer transactions, together with a balance figure.

1 From the Customers window click on the Statements button to bring up the Customer Statements window

You can also use the Customer Statement window to delete statements no longer required, or to modify and design your own statements.

2 Choose the statement layout you require

3 Ensure Preview is checked

4 Click Generate Report to bring up the selection Criteria box

5 Enter Customer Reference range

6 Enter Transaction Date From & To

To preview a sample report, simply enter a small number of records in the box provided.

7 Click OK to preview statement

8 Use the Zoom button on the preview to zoom in or out if you need to check any statement detail

9 When satisfied, click Print to print the statement, then Close all windows

The Supplier Ledger

This chapter shows you how to create and maintain supplier records within the Suppliers (Purchase) Ledger. Through recording invoices and credit notes you receive you can see how much you owe, when these payments are due and any disputed items. You will learn how to view details of any invoices received and payments made to suppliers using tables, graphs and reports.

Covers

Chapter Three

The Supplier Toolbar

The Supplier toolbar has many similar buttons to the Customer toolbar, and again provides you with facilities for setting up records, checking supplier activity, recording invoices, credit notes and reporting.

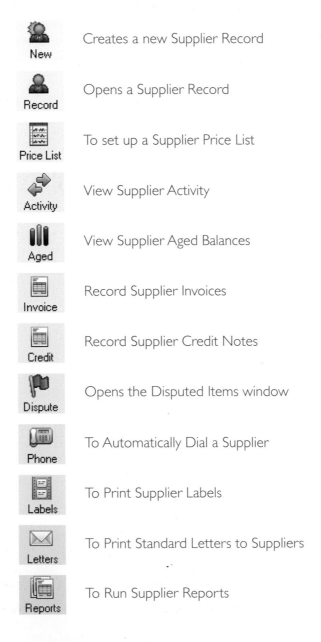

New — Creates a new Supplier Record

Record — Opens a Supplier Record

Price List — To set up a Supplier Price List

Activity — View Supplier Activity

Aged — View Supplier Aged Balances

Invoice — Record Supplier Invoices

Credit — Record Supplier Credit Notes

Dispute — Opens the Disputed Items window

Phone — To Automatically Dial a Supplier

Labels — To Print Supplier Labels

Letters — To Print Standard Letters to Suppliers

Reports — To Run Supplier Reports

Creating Supplier Records

Within this window you can view, edit or delete a supplier record. A new supplier record can also be added if you have all of the details to hand. To add a new supplier first select Suppliers from the Sage Line 50 toolbar, then do the following:

Until you are familiar with Sage Line 50, use the New wizard for simple step-by-step instructions for entering a new supplier record.

1 Select Suppliers from the Line 50 V12 navigation bar

2 Click on Record to bring up the Supplier Record window

3 Use Details to enter supplier information, such as name, address and contact details

4 Use the O/B button to enter an Opening Balance where required

Always start with the Account Code when entering a new record.

5 Use the Credit Control tab to enter any agreed credit terms

6 Select Account Status from this drop down box

7 Enter supplier Bank details for payment transfers

8 Click Save to store the Supplier Record

9 Enter a new record or click Close to finish

Using Search

This useful Search feature is also available within other program windows, such as Customers, Products, Nominal and Invoicing.

The Search function available within the suppliers window can help save you valuable time when searching for specific information regarding supplier transactions. The following example shows you how to produce a list of suppliers you owe money to:

1 Click the Search button in the bottom left hand corner of the Suppliers window to bring up the Search window

2 Click here and select Where

3 Select Balance in this field

4 Select Greater than here

Search - ☒

Only select records from 'Suppliers'

	Join	Field	Condition	Value
	Where	Balance	Is Greater Than	0.00

Account Status
Average Time To Pay
Balance
Balance Current
Balance Future

Expression:

[Wizard] [Discard] [Open] [Save] [Save As]   [Apply] [Close]

To search using part information, select the Is Equal To condition and preceed the Value with the symbol $. For example, use $W1 and the field Account Address Line 5 to search for all Suppliers in the London W1 area.

5 Enter a zero value in this field

6 Click Apply, then Close to return to the Suppliers window

7 Note that only records matching the search are displayed. The title bar indicates Search is applied

8 To cancel the search and show all records, click the icon here

Suppliers   (10 of 16 Records matched) 🔍 Change View ▾ ✕

Supplier Activity

To view this screen from the Supplier Record window, enter the A/C for the supplier required (if none selected) and then click on the Activity tab.

This feature enables you to view each supplier's transactions in detail. If less complete information is required, you can define a transaction or date range to limit the view:

1 From the Suppliers window, click on the supplier you want to look at

Double click on any Purchase Invoice (PI) transaction to bring up the relevant Product Purchase Order.

2 Click on Activity

3 In the next box enter the required range and transaction type

4 Click OK to bring up the Activity window

5 Click here on a transaction for more details

It is useful to note that the following codes indicate the transaction type:

PI = Purchase Invoice
PP = Purchase Payment
PC = Purchase Credit Note
PD = Discount on a Purchase Payment
PA = Purchase Payment on Account

6 Click Close to return to the Suppliers window

Supplier Aged Balance

Aged balance is the term given to the time lapse of outstanding debt, whether owed to you or by you. Sage Line 50 lets you view the amount of money you owe your Suppliers, grouped on the age of the debt. It is common practice for businesses to give 30 days credit, but other terms are sometimes negotiated. Sage Line 50 default aged periods are 30, 60 and 90 days.

1 From the Suppliers window, click on the supplier you require (or ensure none selected to view all) and select the Aged button from the toolbar

2 Enter appropriate dates here

3 Click OK to display the Aged Balances Report

4 To see the transactions which make up the aged balance click Detailed

5 Close each window when finished

Recording Supplier Invoices

Always check the correct tax code has been selected for the VAT to avoid errors later. Sage Line 50 enters T1 (standard rate) for you by default. You may need to change this to T0 for transactions which are zero rated or to T9 for those not involving VAT.

Invoices received from your suppliers can be entered a few at a time using the Batch Supplier Invoices window. You have full flexibility using this option, such as posting each invoice item to a different nominal account if need be, or allocating to a different VAT code, such as from default VAT to zero VAT. To enter invoices, do the following:

1 From the Suppliers window click Invoice to bring up the Batch Supplier Invoices window

2 Type the supplier's account code here or use the Finder button

Remember that with batch invoices, no printouts are generated of the transaction entered. Use activity reports if you require hardcopy.

3 Enter the Date and other invoice details, then check the Nominal (N/C) and Tax (T/C) codes and amend if necessary

4 When all details are correct and all invoices have been entered, click Save to post the details

5 Click Close to return to the Suppliers window

'Posting' means updating the Nominal ledger and relevant supplier's details. If you do not wish to save this batch, choose the Discard button to clear the data and start again.

6 Note that the Supplier's record now displays the new balance, then click Close again

Recording Supplier Credit Notes

Occasionally, goods ordered from suppliers may arrive damaged or incomplete. The supplier issues you a credit note reducing the amount owed. Credit notes are recorded using the Credit option from the Suppliers window.

If a credit note contains a number of items, for your benefit it is advisable to enter each transaction individually, but giving them the same account code, date and reference. Sage Line 50 will group these together and list them as a single credit note. You can then view the note in detail using Activity from the Suppliers window.

1 To record a credit note, from the Suppliers window click Credit

2 Enter the supplier Account Code. Use the Finder button if you don't have the code

3 Enter the credit note date

4 Enter the remaining details and check that they are correct

6 Click Close to return to the Suppliers window

5 Click Save to update the nominal ledger and record the credit details

7 Note that the outstanding balance has changed and click Close

Supplier Letters and Labels

As with Customers, Sage Line 50 includes the facility to produce preformatted letters and labels for your suppliers. You can create whatever standard letters or label layouts you wish. All necessary address information etc. is taken from the stored supplier details.

To produce the standard letter informing suppliers of your change of address, do the following:

The credit control tab window has an option to Restrict mailing. Use this to control who you send mailshots to.

1 From the Suppliers window click Letters to bring up the Supplier Letters window

2 Click on the letter required and ensure Preview is selected

3 Click Generate Report

4 Check the letters and click Print, then OK in the Printer box

Always remember to check that the correct paper, labels and printer type have been selected before printing to avoid wasting time and paper.

5 When finished, Close all windows

Labels

To produce address labels for your suppliers, click the Labels button from the Suppliers window then carry out Steps 2–5 as above.

Supplier Reports

You can generate a wide range of detailed reports on your suppliers. These reports are produced from the information you entered about suppliers and their transactions. Whilst Sage Line 50 already has a considerable number of reports set up, if any further reports are required you can create them using the Report Designer (see Chapter Twelve). To run or view a supplier report:

1 Click on the Reports button in the Suppliers window

2 Click here on the required folder

3 Select the report you require from the Supplier Reports list

4 Select Printer or Preview

5 Click Generate Report to produce report

6 If a Criteria box appears, enter the From and To details, then click OK

7 After printing, Close all windows

The Nominal Ledger

This chapter explains the important role played by the Nominal Ledger and how its accounts detail the flow of money in and out of the business. You will be shown how to analyse these account transactions using tables, graphs and transaction activity reports so you can control and monitor finances through making informed business decisions. You can even tailor your own Nominal Ledger set of accounts to meet specific business needs.

Covers

Chapter Four

The Nominal Toolbar

The Nominal toolbar buttons provide you with facilities for setting up records, viewing account activity, making journal entries, setting up prepayments and accruals, working on the chart of accounts and reporting.

New — Creates a new Nominal Account

Record — Opens a Nominal Record

Activity — View a Nominal Account's Activity

Journals — Enter Journal double-entries

Reversals — Process Nominal Ledger Reversals

Prepay — Enter Nominal Ledger Prepayments

Accrual — Enter Nominal Ledger Accrual

COA — Opens the Chart of Accounts

Reports — To Run Nominal Ledger Reports

The Nominal Ledger

To help you work with the Nominal Ledger, here is the standard nominal accounts for Sage Line 50:

- Asset Accounts from 0001 to 1999
- Liability Accounts from 2000 to 3999
- Income Accounts from 4000 to 4999
- Purchase Accounts from 5000 to 5999
- Direct Expenses from 6000 to 6999
- Overheads from 7000 to 9999

The Nominal Ledger, also referred to as the General Ledger, is a grouped analysis of your sales and purchase transactions. For example, when a sales or purchase invoice is posted to the sales or purchase ledger, Sage Line 50 records it in the Nominal Ledger against the appropriate Nominal account number.

It therefore contains all the accounts for your business, e.g. sales, purchases, expenses, VAT, cash and bank, sundry income, fixed assets, liabilities, capital and owner's drawings. However, it does not keep details of debtors and creditors. These are held in the respective sales and purchase ledgers.

The Nominal accounts let you see quickly where your money is. Information from here is used in the production of management reports to tell you how your business is performing.

A shortcut for bringing up the Nominal Ledger window is to click on the following button in the Sage Line 50 V12 navigation bar:

1 Click Modules from the Line 50 menu bar, then Nominal Ledger

2 Select the Ledger view you prefer

3 Click Close when finished

In Sage Line 50, a standard set of nominal accounts are created upon installation, unless in the Startup Wizard you decided to create your own nominal structure. Note that the latter option only creates the Control Accounts for you.

Nominal Records

You can tailor the nominal accounts to exactly meet your needs by using the Nominal Record window. You have the facility to add, edit and delete nominal accounts as well as viewing transactions posted to each account on a monthly basis.

Using the Record window you can also set budget values for each month of your financial year for a particular nominal account. You can also compare the actual monthly figures against the budget values to keep track of how close you are to meeting targets. To add a nominal account record, do the following:

1 Click Record from the Nominal Ledger to bring up the Nominal Record window

2 In the Details tab box, enter the new nominal account code

You cannot delete a Nominal Code whilst there is still a balance on it.

The New account details must first be saved before you can enter an Opening Balance.

3 Press the Tab key and note that this is a New Account

4 Enter new account Name, Budget and Prior Year values

5 Click Save to store details or Discard to start again

6 Click Close to return to the Nominal Ledger

Viewing Nominal Transactions

You can view your Nominal Ledger transactions by using:

You can save the graph to disk as a chart file. Click on Disk icon and enter a file name.

- Graphs

- Activity reports

- Table formats

 Transaction Analysis using Graphs

A range of 2D and 3D charts is available in Sage Line 50 to visually compare your current year's trading against the previous year and any budgets you have put in place.

1 From the Nominal Ledger window, select the nominal account you wish to view

2 Click Record, then select the Graphs tab to display data in graphical form

You can include Sage Line 50 graphs in other documents you may wish to produce. Simply use the Camera button to copy the graph, open your application and use the paste function to insert it into your other document.

3 To choose a different type of graph, click here, then click on the graph required

4 Click on the Printer button to print out the graph

5 Click Close to return to the Nominal Ledger window

Transactions already cleared from the audit trail are shown as a single carried forward total and displayed as an Opening Balance (O/BAL).

Each line of the Activity list box represents a single invoice, credit note, payment on account or receipt.

Viewing Nominal Account Activity

You will occasionally need to view transactions that have been posted to the nominal ledger accounts. To do this from the Nominal Ledger window:

1 Click on the nominal account you wish to view

2 Click on the Activity button to bring up the Activity Date Range box

3 Enter the appropriate Transaction/Date ranges and Type to Display

4 Click OK to display Activity

5 Click here on a transaction to view any further details

6 Use Previous & Next buttons to view other nominal accounts, if more than one selected in Step 1

You can select more than one account to view at a time. Then simply use the Next and Previous buttons to scroll through them.

7 Click Close to return to the Nominal Ledger

You can tell at a glance if Search is being applied to a list because it will not display the words 'All Records' on the right side of the title bar.

Transaction Codes

Transactions in the Activity window are indicated by a type (Tp) or transaction code, allocated by Sage Line 50. The following is a list of transaction codes used:

BR (Bank Receipt) SD (Discount on Sales Receipt)
BP (Bank Payment) SA (Sales Receipt on Account)
CP (Cash Payment) PI (Purchase Invoice)
CR (Cash Receipt) PP (Purchase Payment)
JD (Journal Debit) PC (Purchase Credit)
JC (Journal Credit) PD (Discount on Purchase Payment)
SI (Sales Invoice) PA (Purchase Payment on Account)
SR (Sales Receipt) VP (Visa Credit Payments)
SC (Sales Credit) VR (Visa Credit Receipts)

Using Search

It is sometimes handy to reduce the number of records displayed in the Nominal Ledger window or on your reports to only those that match a specific criteria. This will save you having to look through too many records just to find the information you need. For example, this is how to list only control accounts in the Nominal Ledger window:

The Number (No.) column shows the transaction number in the Audit Trail. You will need this number if you wish to amend or delete a transaction using the File, Maintenance, Corrections option.

1 Click Search in the Nominal Ledger window

2 Select Where

3 Choose Account Type Code here

Search remains applied to a list until you click the Search icon on the right hand side of the title bar.

4 Select Equal To

5 Select Control Account from the list

6 Click on the Apply button

7 Click Close

The Journal

The rules for debits and credits are: Debit the account which receives the value; Credit the account which gives the value.

The Journal allows you to make transfers between any of your nominal account codes regardless of type (Asset, Liability, Income or Expenditure), provided you adhere to double-entry bookkeeping principles. It lets you enter transactions which may not be covered within the standard Sage Line 50 facilities.

It is a useful source of reference for these non-regular transactions and can reduce errors by providing a list (audit trail) for checking purposes. Examples of these transactions include correction of errors and transfer of monies, as well as the purchase and sale of fixed assets on credit.

As stated, the Journal follows double-entry bookkeeping principles i.e., the value of the credit transaction must equal the value of the debit transaction. Each line of the Journal Entry table represents a single transaction; therefore there must be at least two transactions in the journal (a credit and a debit).

However, this does not mean that you must post a single credit item for every single debit item. You can, for example, post several debits but only one balancing credit, and vice versa. Provided the net difference between your postings is always zero (i.e. the total value of credits equals the total value of debits), you can then post the Journal.

'Skeleton' Journals

For journals that you make regularly, payments from a bank to a credit card account for example, Sage Line 50 lets you save the details of that journal entry so that you can use it the next time without having to enter it all again. This is called a 'skeleton'. Some skeleton journals were set up at installation, such as the VAT Liability Transfer Journal.

If you post a journal entry incorrectly, Sage Line 50 lets you use the Reversals button from the Journals toolbar to remove the entry. You can then simply re-enter the journal correctly. Just click on the Reversals button and follow the prompts to print the Nominal Ledger Day Book and backup your data before you process the reversal.

To save a skeleton journal, click on the Memorise button after you have set up the journal. To load a skeleton journal, click on the Recall button, select the journal you need and click on the Load button. You can even load one of the skeleton journals provided by Line 50, modify it to suit your needs, then save it.

Reversals

In Line 50 V12 you can reverse an incorrectly posted journal entry. Use Sage Help for a full explanation of reversing a journal.

Reversals

Making a Journal Entry

Here is an example of how you would make a journal entry for a transfer of funds between your bank account and business building society account.

When you make a manual journal entry, VAT is neither calculated for you nor posted to the VAT control account.

1 From the Nominal Ledger toolbar, click Journals

2 Use the Calendar button if a different date is required

If you use a journal entry regularly save it as a Skeleton using the Memorise button, so you can re-create it quickly and easily later.

Memorise

3 Enter details for both the credit and debit transactions. Reference is optional

4 Note, the default Tax code of T9 is entered for you by Sage Line 50

6 To process your journal click Save, or Discard to cancel

5 Check total Debit and Credit are equal and a zero balance is displayed in the Balance box

7 Click Close to return to Nominal Ledger window

Before saving the Journal, always ensure the Balance box shows zero. If the value of the credit transactions does not equal the value of the debit transactions, then Sage Line 50 issues a warning and will not let you save the Journal.

Note that Sage Line 50 will not automatically calculate VAT, or post it to the VAT Control Account. If VAT is required, enter each VAT element as a separate line, with a debit or credit to the appropriate VAT Control Account.

Setting up Prepayments

Just click on the Wizard button to let the Prepayments Wizard guide you through setting up a prepayment:

Wizard

To adjust statements and reports for any payments which have to be made in advance, for example rent or insurance, there is a Prepayments option available from the Nominal Ledger window. This allows for a payment to be shown as spread over the number of months it refers to, not just the month it was paid in.

After setting up a prepayment, when you run the Month End procedure the correct monthly figure is posted to the appropriate account. All you have to do is to remember to post a suitable payment for the full amount (i.e. from the bank) to the appropriate nominal account.

Use Key F6 to save time and reduce errors when copying data from a previous transaction entry.

1 From the Nominal Ledger toolbar, click Prepay to bring up the Prepayments window

2 Enter relevant nominal account code or use the Finder button

3 Enter the details here

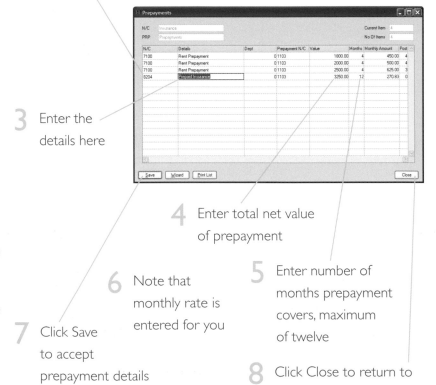

4 Enter total net value of prepayment

No accounting takes place when prepayment details are saved. Journal Entry postings are only made when the Month End, Post Prepayments option is run.

6 Note that monthly rate is entered for you

5 Enter number of months prepayment covers, maximum of twelve

7 Click Save to accept prepayment details

8 Click Close to return to Nominal Ledger window

Setting up Accruals

The Accruals option allows the accounts to be adjusted for any payments you make in one accounting period which in fact relate to a previous period, such as a gas or electricity bill.

In this example, the transaction would be entered using the Accrual and Gas or Electricity accounts. When the charges actually fall due and the bill is paid, the payment transaction is applied to the Accrual account, not the Gas or Electricity account.

As with the prepayments option, the accruals are posted as part of your month end procedure using the Period End, Month End option. This procedure automatically updates the audit trail and nominal accounts records.

No accounting takes place when accrual details are saved. Journal Entry postings are only made when the Month End, Post Accruals option is run.

2 Enter relevant nominal account code, or use the Finder button

1 From the Nominal Ledger window click Accrual

3 Enter details

4 Enter the estimated total net value of accrual here

If you have already set up some Accrual entries, these appear in the Accruals window when it opens. Just add your new Accrual at the end of the list.

6 Monthly accrual is calculated for you

5 Enter number of months for the accrual

7 Click Save to accept accrual details

8 Click Close to return to Nominal Ledger window

The Chart of Accounts

During installation, Sage Line 50 created a simple Chart of Accounts suitable for standard reporting, such as Profit and Loss, Balance Sheet, Budget and Prior Year Reports.

It may be that the default account names are not suitable for your business, so the Chart of Accounts can be customised to meet your business requirements. New category types can be introduced into the accounts or current categories edited to reflect, for example, the actual items sold within your business.

The chart of Accounts is subdivided into the following default report category types:

Profit & Loss
- *Sales*
- *Purchases*
- *Direct Expenses*
- *Overheads*

Balance Sheet
- *Fixed Assets*
- *Current Assets*
- *Current Liabilities*
- *Long Term Liabilities*
- *Capital & Reserves*

1 To examine the Chart of Accounts' facilities, click COA from the Nominal Ledger window

2 If you want to look at a chart, select it from the list and click Edit

Always check that the name of the layout you selected appears automatically in the 'Current' text box.

3 To create a new Chart of Accounts, click the Add button

4 To use a particular Chart of Accounts simply highlight it from the list and click the Current button

5 When finished, click Close to return to the Nominal Ledger window

Creating a Chart of Accounts Layout

Do the following to add a new Chart of Accounts layout:

1 Click COA from the Nominal Ledger window

2 Click Add in the Chart of Accounts window

3 Enter name of your new Chart of Accounts layout

4 Click Add to continue

5 Click on a category and change its description to that required in your financial reports

6 Enter (or amend) the headings for each range of nominal accounts in the selected category

7 Set range of nominal accounts to be included for each selected category in Low & High boxes

Use the Check button to quickly find any nominal account errors in your new layout.

8 Click Check to see if you've made any errors

9 Click Save, or Close to discard

10 To print your Chart of Accounts, click Print, then Run

11 Select required chart in the Criteria box

12 Click OK to print

Nominal Reports

To print or preview reports using the nominal data already entered into the system, use the Reports option from the Nominal Ledger. Sage Line 50 already supplies a considerable number of pre-installed reports to suit most needs, but you can create additional custom reports using the Report Designer. See Chapter 12 for more details on creating reports.

Use the Criteria button on the Nominal Ledger window to make report generation easier by restricting the selection of nominal account codes to specified criteria.

To print a Nominal Ledger report, do the following:

1 From the Nominal Ledger toolbar, click Reports

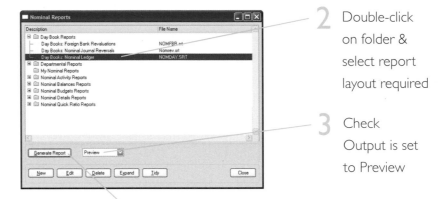

2 Double-click on folder & select report layout required

3 Check Output is set to Preview

4 Click Generate Report to bring up the Criteria box

You may sometimes find it easier to select nominal accounts from the Nominal Ledger window instead of entering them in the Criteria box.

5 Type range details or use the Calendar and Finder buttons

6 Click OK to preview report

7 If a printout is required, click on the Print button

8 Click Close to return to the Layout window

9 Close all windows to finish

The Bank

This chapter shows you how to maintain your bank account records and transactions. This includes deposits, payments, transfer of money between bank accounts and adjustments to show bank charges and interest received. It also covers reconciling your statements, processing recurring entries and the automatic production of cheques.

Covers

The Bank Toolbar

This toolbar provides features for the recording and maintenance of bank transactions and records. You can perform adjustments, record the transfer of monies, enter receipts, produce statements and reports and even print cheques.

 To quickly create a new Bank account, use the New Wizard from the Bank Toolbar and work through the simple step by step screens.

New

Record — Opens a Bank Record

Reconcile — Opens Bank Account Reconciliation

Payment — Record Bank Payments

Supplier — Record Supplier Payments

Remittance — To Print Bank Remittances

Batch — To Record a Batch Purchase Payment

Receipt — Record Money Received

Customer — Record Customer Receipts

Transfer — Make Bank Transfers

Recurring — Opens Recurring Entries Window

Cash Flow — Opens the Cash Flow Window

Statement — To Print Bank Statements

Cheques — To Print Cheques

Reports — To Run Bank Account Reports

Bank Accounts

There are three types of Bank accounts used in Sage Line 50: the Bank Account, Cash Account and Credit Card Account.

The arrows on the Customers toolbar let you scroll across all available buttons.

The Bank account option treats both Bank and Building Societies as bank accounts. Three bank accounts have been automatically set up to include a bank current account, a bank deposit account and a building society account.

A single Cash Account called Petty Cash has been set up, but other cash accounts can be added, for example, Emergency Cash or Additional Travel Expenses etc.

The facility to record your credit card bank details is available and allows you to monitor any credit card transactions you have made and keep track of your money. Two credit card accounts have already been set up for use.

To view the Bank account window:

1 Select Bank from the Line 50 V12 navigation bar

Have your current bank balance to hand when creating new Bank records.

2 Click on the bank account required, then click on the appropriate icon for the function you wish to carry out

3 When finished, click Close

Bank, Cash and Credit Accounts

Sage Line 50 provides three types of bank accounts:

Refer to Chapter 13 for more information on entering your opening balances.

- **Bank Account** (includes both bank deposit and current account, plus a building society account).

- **Cash Account** (named Petty Cash).

- **Credit Card Account** (company credit card and credit card receipts).

These accounts can be edited to match your own details. Accounts can also be added or deleted. To set up your Bank account details:

1 From the Bank Accounts window, select account type required and click on the Record icon

2 Make changes if necessary here

3 Click here to enter Current Balance. The Opening Balance Setup box appears

Your bank accounts and financial reports use nominal codes 1200 to 1299.

6 Click Bank Details tab and enter further details

4 Enter Opening Balance and other details

5 Click Save

Should the minimum balance fall below the figure entered, it will be displayed in red in the Bank Accounts window.

7 Click Save to store details, then Close

Recording Bank Payments

Payments to your suppliers should be entered using the Supplier option as this brings up any outstanding invoices when the supplier's account reference is entered.

For recording any non-invoiced or one-off payments use the Payment option from the Bank Accounts window. Sage Line 50 then makes it very easy for you to keep track of where your money goes – simply select the appropriate account, enter the payment and post it.

To record Bank payments:

1 Click Payment from the Bank Accounts window

2 Use Finder button to enter Bank account code

3 Enter Date (and transaction Reference if required)

If you only know the Gross value of the payment, simply enter it in the Net box and click on the Calc. Net button.

4 Enter a Nominal Code for the payment to be posted to, or use the Finder button

5 Enter Details

Use the Discard button if you want to clear any data already entered and start again. Any entries already saved will not be cancelled.

6 Enter amount (change Tax Code from default of T1 if necessary)

7 Click Save to post details (update the nominal ledger and the Bank account)

8 Click Close to finish

Supplier Invoice Payments

Leave the cheque number blank if you intend using the Cheques option. Cheques will be automatically generated for you.

The Supplier option from the Bank Accounts toolbar will provide you with a detailed transaction list of any outstanding invoice items, credit notes and payments made on account to suppliers. To record payment of a supplier invoice do the following:

1 In the Bank Accounts window, select the account required (e.g. Bank Current Account) and click the Supplier button

2 Enter supplier account code

3 Use Calendar button if payment date is different

Enter a discount value in the discount box, not a percentage, for any invoiced item. The Analysis Total box decreases by the discount value entered.

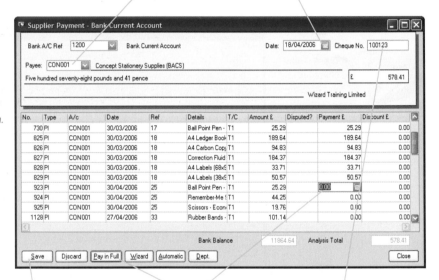

Supplier Payment - Bank Current Account

Bank A/C Ref 1200   Bank Current Account   Date: 18/04/2006   Cheque No. 100123

Payee: CON001   Concept Stationery Supplies (BACS)

Five hundred seventy-eight pounds and 41 pence   £ 578.41

     Wizard Training Limited

No.	Type	A/c	Date	Ref	Details	T/C	Amount £	Disputed?	Payment £	Discount £
730	PI	CON001	30/03/2006	17	Ball Point Pen -	T1	25.29		25.29	0.00
825	PI	CON001	30/03/2006	18	A4 Ledger Book	T1	189.64		189.64	0.00
826	PI	CON001	30/03/2006	18	A4 Carbon Copy	T1	94.83		94.83	0.00
827	PI	CON001	30/03/2006	18	Correction Fluid	T1	184.37		184.37	0.00
828	PI	CON001	30/03/2006	18	A4 Labels (68x9	T1	33.71		33.71	0.00
829	PI	CON001	30/03/2006	18	A4 Labels (38x9	T1	50.57		50.57	0.00
923	PI	CON001	30/04/2006	25	Ball Point Pen -	T1	25.29		0.00	0.00
924	PI	CON001	30/04/2006	25	Remember-Me S	T1	44.25		0.00	0.00
925	PI	CON001	30/04/2006	25	Scissors - Econ	T1	19.76		0.00	0.00
1128	PI	CON001	27/04/2006	33	Rubber Bands -	T1	101.14		0.00	0.00

Bank Balance 11864.64   Analysis Total 578.41

Save   Discard   Pay in Full   Wizard   Automatic   Dept.   Close

5 Enter value in Payment box for part-payment or click on Pay in Full button to enter full amount

4 Enter cheque number if required (See the first DON'T FORGET icon in the margin)

6 Repeat Step 5 for any remaining transactions

Use the Remittance button on the Bank toolbar to quickly print a batch of remittances:

Remittance

7 Click Save to save payment details and Close

Batch Purchase Payments

You can pay a transaction in full or part.

You can list all outstanding purchase invoices, purchase credit notes and purchase payments on account for all suppliers using the Batch option from the Bank Accounts window. The transactions are sorted firstly by supplier and then by transaction number.

Outstanding transactions can be paid in three ways:

- All transactions paid in full.

- Individual transactions paid in full.

- Individual transactions paid in part.

To record full or part payments:

All outstanding transactions can be paid in full in one go using the Pay All button, but there will only be one posting.

1 From Bank Accounts select the account and click Batch

2 To pay ALL outstanding transactions click Pay All

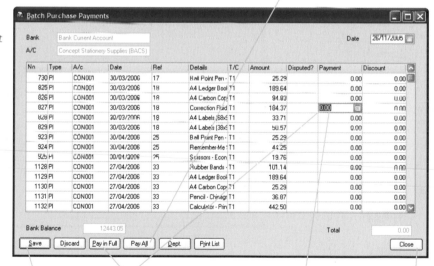

If any of the selected transactions are in dispute Sage line 50 displays a warning message.

3 To make INDIVIDUAL full payments, select a transaction and click on the Pay in Full button

4 For a PART PAYMENT simply enter the amount in the Payment box

5 When finished click Save, or Discard to start again

6 Click Close

Bank Receipts

If you select a Company Credit Card Account (rather than a Credit Card Receipts account), Sage Line 50 warns you that the account you selected is usually for payments only and vice versa. You can turn off this warning on the Company Preferences' Parameters tab.

To record any non-invoiced or miscellaneous payments you receive, the Receipts option from the Bank Accounts window is used. These items are allocated a specific nominal code for analysis purposes so a check can be made on monies received.

To enter receipt of money:

1 From the Bank Account window Click on the Receipt icon

2 In the Bank Receipts window, select the appropriate Bank account

3 Ensure the required Date is entered here

4 Enter a Reference here, such as a cheque number

If you only have the Gross value to hand, enter it in the Net box and click on Calc. Net.

A receipt reference, i.e. cheque number or deposit number, will help when reconciling bank accounts.

5 Select a Nominal Account Code to post the receipt to and give details

6 Enter Net value

7 Repeat Steps 2–6 to record further receipts, then click Save to post transactions

8 When finished, Close all windows

Recording Customer Receipts

The Customer option from the Bank Accounts window is used to record money received from your customers. When the customer's account reference is entered, any outstanding invoices appear automatically in the Customer Receipt window.

To record full or part payments:

You can pay an invoice in full or part but you cannot allocate an amount more than the item value.

1 From the Bank Accounts window, select the bank account required and click Customer

2 Enter a customer Account Code to display all items not fully paid for that customer

3 Change Date if necessary and enter a paying in Reference, if possible

Use the Customers Receipt Wizard to help you record any cheques received for customer invoice payments, allocate credit notes and payments on account to invoices or to post a payment on account only.

No.	Type	A/c	Date	Ref	Details	T/C	Amount £	Disputed?	Receipt £	Discount £
660	SI	CGS001	07/03/2006	36	Filing Cabinet - 5	T1	144.57		144.57	0.00
661	SI	CGS001	07/03/2006	36	Mouse Mat - (24	T1	4.99		4.99	0.00
662	SI	CGS001	07/03/2006	36	Mailing Bag Bu	T1	33.36		33.36	0.00
663	SI	CGS001	07/03/2006	36	Copy Paper - St	T1	321.92		321.92	0.00
664	SI	CGS001	07/03/2006	36	Ball Point Pen -	T1	22.24		22.24	0.00
665	SI	CGS001	07/03/2006	36	Ball Point Pen -	T1	8.90		0.00	0.00
666	SI	CGS001	07/03/2006	36	I P200 Laser Pri	T1	1334.51		0.00	0.00
667	SI	CGS001	07/03/2006	36	LP200 Laser Pri	T1	40.04		0.00	0.00
668	SI	CGS001	07/03/2006	36	Carriage	T1	117.50		0.00	0.00

Bank A/C Ref: 1200 Name: Bank Current Account
A/C: CGS001 Name: County Golf Supplies
Date: 20/04/2006 Reference: 100992
Amount: 527.08

Bank Balance: 12970.13 Analysis Total: 527.08

Save | Discard | Pay in Full | Wizard | Automatic | Dept. | Close

Sage Line 50 automatically warns you of any disputed items.

4 If FULL payment has been received select a transaction and click Pay in Full

5 If this is a PART payment enter the amount received here

6 Enter any further receipts then click Save to process them or Discard to start again

7 When finished, Close all windows

Bank Transfers

Sometimes you will need to transfer money from one bank account to another. You can record this using the Transfer option from the Bank Accounts window or by making a journal entry.

You can also record a Bank Transfer through a journal entry.

To make a bank transfer do the following:

1 From the Bank Accounts window, select the bank you wish to move the money from

2 Click Transfer to open the Bank Transfer window

3 Enter Nominal Code of the Bank you are transferring to

4 Enter a Reference and appropriate Details

Sage Line 50 always enters today's date in the Date box for you, but this can be altered if necessary.

5 Check that the correct date is entered in the Date box

7 Click Save to process the transfer or Discard to start again

6 Enter transfer amount

8 Click Close to finish, then Close again

Recurring Entries

For payments which remain consistent and are paid on a monthly basis, for example rent and electricity, the Recurring option can be used from the Bank Accounts window. This feature is also useful for standing orders and direct debits and prevents payments such as these from being overlooked. Each month, these transactions need posting to update your banks and ledgers.

If there are any outstanding recurring entries, Sage Line 50 reminds you on startup and asks if you wish to post them. To add a recurring entry:

Recurring entries need processing each month before you can run the Month or Year End procedures.

Sage Line 50 will only let you post journal credits when you post journal debits of the same value, and vice versa.

The Last Posted box always remains blank until the new entry is saved and processed.

To stop a monthly payment, click the Suspend Posting box. This is handy for those payments which do not need posting every month.

1 Select Recurring from the Bank Accounts window and Click Add

2 Enter transaction type from the list box

3 Enter the Bank Account Code

4 Enter a Nominal Code to post the transaction to

5 Give Transaction Reference/Details as required and enter Posting Frequency

6 Enter Net amount and check the Tax Code

7 Click OK to return to the Recurring Entries window

8 Click Process and Process All to process the recurring entries, then click Close to finish

Generating Cheques

This is a relatively recent feature within Sage Line 50 and offers the ability to print cheques automatically for a particular bank account. All Purchase Payments (type PP) and Purchase Payments on Account (type PA) transactions not previously printed and with blank references are listed in the Print Cheques window. This is how to print cheques using the cheque generator:

If no transactions are selected, the program will print cheques for ALL the transactions.

1 From the Bank Accounts window, select the required bank account and click on the Cheques button

2 Allocate a new Cheque Number if required

You can now print a cheque for a supplier without first having to set up an account.

3 Select transactions requiring cheques

4 Click Print Cheques

5 Select layout required, then click Run

6 Click Yes if cheques printed correctly, then Close

The Bank Statement

Sage Line 50 provides you with the facility to print your bank statements out at any time, showing all reconciled bank payments and receipts.

To use this facility effectively, you should make sure that you enter all Bank transactions accurately and completely so that the Sage Line 50 Bank statements match your actual bank statements.

These statements show the transactions made to and from each bank account, and prove useful for cross-referencing purposes when checking for any transaction omissions or additions. To print a report in bank statement format, do the following:

1 From the Bank Accounts window click on the Statement button

2 Select Preview from Output options and Click Run

3 Enter Transaction Date range

You can also save the Bank Statement reports as a file for use at a later date. Simply click on the Save As button in the report preview window.

4 Enter To and From Bank Ref's, using the Finder button for case

5 Click OK to preview statement

6 Click Print and OK from the print dialog box

To bring up previously saved statements, click Open and select the required statement from the list.

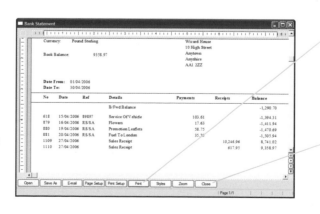

7 Click Close when finished

Bank Account Reconciliation

Bank reconciliation is the process of matching up your computer bank records and transactions with those shown on the statements received from your bank.

Before you select any transactions to reconcile, always check that the opening balance shown in the Bank Reconciliation window is the same as the opening balance on your actual bank statement.

The Bank Reconciliation window displays transactions which have not been previously reconciled. After entering the date of the statement, you can work through your bank statement matching the transactions recorded in Sage Line 50. If necessary, you should make any adjustments needed to ensure that Sage Line 50 bank accounts accurately reflect the transactions processed by your actual bank. To reconcile a bank account:

1 From the Bank Accounts window select the bank account to be reconciled, then click Reconcile

2 Enter the closing balance of your bank statement

3 Enter date of the bank statement

4 Complete the details, then Click OK

A bank account cannot be reconciled if the check box No Bank Reconciliation has been selected on the bank record.

5 Click on each transaction that matches on the bank statement

6 Click on Match Transaction to add marked transactions to lower window

7 If the Reconcile and Statement End balances match, click Save

8 Click Close

Thoroughly check all transactions on the bank statement against the Bank Reconciliation list. Also check that the Reconcile Balance box matches the closing balance of your bank statement.

Bank reconciliation will only work correctly provided that a number of important rules are followed:

- The opening balance shown on the Bank Reconciliation window must match the opening balance on your actual bank statement.

If for some reason they are different, you will need to check why and make the necessary adjustments. One way of doing this is to view the selected bank's activity from within the nominal ledger. To see if a transaction has been reconciled, check the Bank column in the Audit Trail, where R = reconciled and N = not reconciled.

As you select each transaction note that the Reconcile Balance value automatically changes.

- Work through your actual bank statement progressively one line at a time, clicking on the corresponding transaction entry in the Bank reconciliation window to highlight it.

- If you come across a transaction on your bank statement not shown in Sage Line 50, you should record this transaction immediately using the Adjustments facility.

- Check everything carefully. When you are satisfied that all necessary transactions for reconciliation have been selected and any adjustments made, the Difference box should show zero.

Making Adjustments

Use the Adjustments button or Bank Payments, Receipts and Transfers to record any additional transactions shown on your bank statement, e.g. bank charges, cashpoint withdrawals etc.

1 From the Reconciliation window, click the Add Adjustment button

2 Enter the Nominal Code of the account to receive the adjustment

3 Enter adjustment details

4 If correct click Save, then Close

Bank Reports

There is a wide range of ready-to-use bank reports provided by Sage Line 50. These reports outline your bank details and transactions and help you keep track of your bank finances. It is advisable that you regularly print out the standard reports, such as Day Books, once you have entered the relevant transactions.

When you have become familiar with the various reports you can save time by sending them straight to the printer without the need to preview. Select Printer instead of Preview in Step 3.

1 From the Bank Accounts window, click Reports to bring up the Bank Reports window

2 Double-click on a folder and select the report required

You can save a report as a file in a number of useful formats, such as Microsoft Write, Text file or Comma Separated Value (CSV).

3 Ensure Preview is selected

4 Click Generate Report to bring up the Criteria window, enter Criteria, click OK and then Print

Cash Flow Window

A new feature in Line 50 is the display of any outstanding payments, receipts and recurring entries. Just click the Cash Flow button.

If you chose to print the report, the Windows Print dialog box appears. Use this to select which pages to print and change your printer settings if necessary.

Cash Flow

For more details see Sage Help. Click Print if required

Products

This chapter shows you how to create and maintain records for products you buy and sell and how to set up product codes. These details, once recorded in the system, will be entered automatically for you when creating sales orders, purchase orders and invoices. You will learn how to monitor stock levels as well as the movement of stock and analyse product transactions using tables, graphs and reports.

Covers

Chapter Six

The Products Toolbar

The Products toolbar provides features for the recording and maintenance of product records and transactions. You have the facility to record the movement of your products and make any adjustments and/or transfer of stock. Product activity can be analysed and reports generated.

To quickly create a new Product record, use the New Wizard from the Product Toolbar and work through the simple step by step screens.

New

Record	Opens a Product Record
Prices	To Set up a Price List
Activity	View a Product Activity
Shortfall	To Run the Product Shortfall Generator
In	Make Stock In Adjustments
Out	Make Stock Out Adjustments
Transfer	Record Stock Transfers
Stk Take	Automatically Make Stock Adjustments
Chk BOM	Check Make-Up Capability For Stock
Returns	For Recording Stock Returns
Allocate	For Recording Stock Allocations
Labels	To Produce Product Labels
Reports	To Run Product Reports

The Product Record

Sage Line 50 allows you to create, edit or delete records for all the products your business sells. Once these records have been set up all you need to do is enter a product code and the details will be automatically included for you on any product invoice, credit note or order you create.

Opening Balances need setting up for your products. Follow the same procedures as for your customers, suppliers, nominal and bank accounts.

From the Product Record window you can view the sales price and quantity in stock for each product. Use the Products option to:

- Create and maintain records for all products bought or sold.

- Record product movements.

- Analyse product transactions using tables or graphs.

- Set up a Bill of Materials.

Once a product record has been set up, take care before deleting it, even if there is zero stock and no more is expected. It may still belong to a part allocated order.

- Keep track of your stock levels.

From the Product Record window you can view the Sales Price and Quantity in stock for each product, together with the Product Code and Description.

1 Select Products from the Line 50 V12 navigation bar

2 To view Product details, select the product and click on Record

Use the Stock Take option to make adjustments to your stock levels after you have completed a stock take. All you need to do is enter the current stock levels for your products and Sage Line 50 makes all of the necessary adjustments for you.

3 To finish click Close

Entering a product record

You can update the sales price for all product items using the Global Changes option from the Tools menu. You can increase or decrease the price by a sum or a percentage.

1 From the Products window click on Record

2 Type a unique Product Code here and press Tab

3 Enter a Description and other relevant details here

4 Choose a Nominal sales account for this product

5 Select correct VAT code

6 Enter Sales Price here

If the Ignore Stock Levels check box is selected (ticked) on the product record, its details will not appear on some reports, i.e. Stock History.

7 Click on O/B button then Yes to save changes

8 Check for correct Date

9 Enter Quantity

10 Enter Cost Price of the Product

You can save your stock take details to a file for opening at a later date, to continue with the stock take, or to view the adjustments that you previously made. Remember, however, to enter all of your stock take details before you process any transactions that would alter your stock levels. This is because your stock details may change between the date that the last stock date was saved and the next time it is re-opened.

11 Click Save

12 Enter any remaining details on the Product Record

13 Click Save to keep the record, or Discard to abort

14 Click Close to return to the Products window

Entering details onto the Product Record

Whilst the Product Record has been designed to accept a considerable amount of detail, not every item is applicable to all products. However, to make reporting more accurate later, you should try and include as much detail as possible about a product when adding records.

Not all of the boxes on the Product Record will accept user entry though. Sage Line 50 calculates or generates the following information and enters it for you. It cannot be directly edited.

If stock level falls below the re-order level, the item appears red in the Products window and also appears on the Re-order report.

Allocated	This figure shows the quantity of the product which has been partly or fully allocated on the sales order, but which has not yet been despatched.
Free Stock	Sage Line 50 calculates the Free Stock as being the In Stock total minus the Allocated stock total.
On Order	Using the Purchase Orders option, this is the quantity of the product which has been put 'on order'.
Last Ord Qty	This shows the amount of stock ordered when the last purchase order for this product was put 'on order'.
Last Ord Date	This shows the date of the last purchase order raised for this product after it had been put on order.
Cost Price	This is the latest cost price for the product item, entered using the Opening Balance option, the Adjustments In option, Purchase Order Processing or the Global Changes option (useful for updating cost prices for all or selected product items).

If you do not enter a Cost Price in the Opening Product Setup box, the product cost is recorded as zero. This could affect your finance reports later.

When running financial or management reports, you must remember that Sage Line 50 will use this latest price even though products already in stock may have actually cost more or less. This may, on occasion, give distorted figures, such as when calculating the total cost value of a product item in stock.

Product Defaults

To save time and make the process of creating new product records easier, Sage Line 50 has the facility to set up certain product defaults.

Whenever a new product record is created, certain regular details, e.g. Nominal Code, Tax Code, Department etc, are asked for. If you use a recording system where these codes remain the same for most of your products, default settings can be set up which will then appear automatically in each new product record without you having to enter them every time. To set up product defaults:

If you set the Unit DP to a value greater than 2, the net amount on any product invoice you create will still be rounded to 2 decimal places.

1 From the Sage Line 50 menu bar, select Settings, then Product Defaults

2 Enter the Nominal Code to be used by default whenever you create orders and product invoices

3 Select the VAT rate & Purchase code from the drop-down list boxes

Product Defaults

Details | Descriptions

Defaults

Sales Nominal Code	4000
Tax Code	T1 17.50
Purchase Nominal Code	
Unit of Sale	Each
Category	1 Paper Products
Department	7 Production
Image Options	Maintain Image Size

Decimal Precision

Quantity D.P.	2
Unit D.P.	2

OK | Cancel

4 Describe the unit of sale here, e.g. 'each', 'box'

5 Select Category and Department as required

6 Enter number of decimal places for quantities

Use the Descriptions tab to quickly set up your own product discount names.

7 Enter number of decimal places for your product sales prices

8 Click OK to save or Cancel to discard any changes

Using Search

Using Search speeds up the process of searching for specific product records, for example to show products which match a particular description, or those with a stock level that has fallen below the required re-order level. The following example shows how to set up a search to restrict Product Records to only those with less than 50 in stock:

The calculator button is a handy way of making an entry in the Value field.

1 Click the Search button in the bottom left hand corner of the Products window to bring up the Search window

Use the Save button to record searches you use frequently. You can then recall these as required from the Search window.

2 Click here and select Where

3 Select Quantity in stock in this field

4 Select Is Less Than here

5 Enter a value of 50 in this field

6 Click Apply, then Close to return to the Products window

Search remains applied to a list until you click the search icon on the right hand side of the title bar:

7 Note that only records matching the search are displayed. The title bar indicates Search is applied

8 To cancel the search and show all records, click the icon here

Products   (82 of 106 Records matched) • Change View ▼   ✕

Bill of Materials

Use the Transfer button from the Products window to increase the stock levels of your product assemblies.

This term relates to a product you hold in stock made up from other products you keep. The made up product is sometimes known as a product assembly and is said to have a Bill of Materials. For example, a first aid kit is a product assembly consisting of various components – bandages, tablets, plasters, cream etc.

For businesses selling a product made up of other products, it is useful to set up a Bill of Materials. In Sage Line 50 this feature keeps track of stock levels and can automatically calculate how many products you can make up for sale from the stock you hold and at what cost price. To set up a Bill of Materials for a product do the following:

The Bill of Materials table itemises each individual component for the product assembly.

1 From the Products window, select the product you wish to set up a Bill of Materials for, then click Record

2 Click the BOM tab from the Product Record

3 Enter Product Code for each item

See how many product assemblies you can make up by looking in the Available to Makeup box.

4 Enter quantity required for product assembly

5 Click Refresh to see how many you can make

6 Click Save to store Bill of Materials, or Discard to start again

7 Click Close

Viewing Transactions

To amend values for all, or a selected group of products within the Product Record, select the Global Changes option from the Tools menu.

The Sales Tab

You can use this dialog box to view the sales value and quantity sold for your selected product during the financial year on a month by month basis. With a record selected:

1 From the Product Record click on the Sales tab

2 Use scroll bar to view different months

Use a range of 2D and 3D chart types to compare how you did last year with this years budget.

3 Click Close

Product Discounts

1 From the Product Record click on the Discount tab

Use the Copy Matrix button to copy the discount structure from another discounted product.

2 Enter quantity for customer to qualify for a discount

3 Enter % Discount

4 Discounted value is calculated for you

6 Click Save to store entries, then Close

5 Repeat as required

Product Activity

Where activities have been cleared at the month end, they will be shown as carried forward totals with a Ref. of O/BAL, usually at the top of the list.

Details regarding adjustments of goods in and out, stock transfers, current quantities in stock, on order and allocated prove invaluable when trying to fulfil orders or analyse and track stock movement.

You can decide when you no longer wish to retain certain transactions on your system by using the Clear Stock option. This facility enables transactions to be cleared from your Product History prior to a specific date.

It is important that you understand the following terms when trying to calculate the availability of stock and to understand the product reports produced by Sage Line 50:

Tp: A code to identify the type of transaction, where:

To clear stock transactions, choose the Period End option from the Tools menu and click the Clear Stock option. Adjustments made are brought forward as opening balances, showing quantities used, in AI and MI.

AI	=	Adjustment In
AO	=	Adjustment Out
MI	=	Movement In (product transfer only)
MO	=	Movement Out (product transfer only)
GR	=	Goods Returned (via credit notes)
GO	=	Goods Out (via sales orders and product invoices)
GI	=	Goods In (via purchase orders)
DI	=	Damages In
DO	=	Damages Out
WO	=	Write Off

Use the type code WO for recording faulty goods as write-offs.

Used: This is the sum of all the AO (Adjustments Out), GO (Goods Out) and MO (Movements Out) quantities for the product within the specified date range.

Cost: If the transaction line refers to an AI (Adjustment In), GI (Goods In), GR (Goods Returned) or MI (Movement In), this shows the cost price.

Sale: Where a transaction line refers to an AO (Adjustment Out), GO (Goods Out) or GR (Goods Returned), this shows the sales price.

...cont'd

Viewing a product's activity is also available using the Activity tab from the Product Record window.

Qty on Order: This is the product quantity which has been placed on order using the Purchase Order option, but not yet delivered.

Qty Allocated: This shows the product quantity that has been allocated to sales orders using the Sales Order Processing option.

Qty in Stock: This is the sum of all the AI (Adjustments In), MI (Movements In), GI (Goods In) and GR (Goods Received), less the quantity used for the specified period.

Qty Available: The Quantity in Stock less Quantity Allocated.

To view Activity from the Products window:

Use the Transaction Type range facility in the Date Range window to refine and speed up your search of Product activity.

1 Click on the product or products required

2 Click on Activity to bring up the Date Range box

3 Enter From and To dates

4 Click OK

Use the Finder button to select another Product Code if required.

5 Click Range to enter new Date Range

6 Click Close when finished

Product Adjustments

If there is a discrepancy after a stock take, enter the stock adjustment using the Stock Take option.

The In and Out options from the Product window are used to record adjustments to your product's stock levels, such as when stock is received into stores, an order is returned, or stock is taken out as damaged.

The In button is used to enter any increase in a product's available stock, whilst the Out option is for recording a decrease.

To make Adjustments In

1 From the Products window click the In option

2 Enter Product Code

3 Enter quantity in

Cost prices are important to the valuation of the stock as product levels are controlled on a first in, first out basis. Always enter cost prices, therefore, to achieve accurate valuation reporting.

4 Enter Date & Ref

5 Enter Cost if changed

6 Click Save to store changes and Close

The Out button is used to record any miscellaneous product movements which decrease a product's available stock level and where no product invoice has been raised.

To make Adjustments Out

You cannot use the Returns option for non-stock or service items.

1 Click the Out option

2 Enter Product Code

3 Enter quantity and click Save and Close

Product Transfers

You can only use a product code which has been previously set up to be a product assembly using the BOM option.

This feature is used for increasing the In Stock quantity of Product Assemblies using components currently in stock. The Product Assemblies are set up using the Bill of Materials option (see page 80).

When using the Stock Transfers option the cost price for each Product Assembly is calculated for you by Sage Line 50, by adding together the cost price of each component.

To make a product transfer from the Products window:

If you do not have sufficient stock of components to make up the quantity you have entered, Sage Line 50 will display a warning.

1 Click on the Transfer button

2 Click on the Product Code Finder button

3 Select Product Assembly Code

4 Click OK

Quickly check your component stock levels by clicking on the Shortfall button on the Products toolbar to bring up the Shortfall Generator window (Accountant Plus and Financial Controller only).

Shortfall

Use Check BOM to quickly check which stock items and components are needed to complete orders.

5 Check Details and Date

6 Enter Quantity required here

7 Click Save to record entries or Discard to start again

8 Click Close

Product Reports

The Stock Reports option allows you to print out a wide range of useful pre-prepared product related reports. These reports show such things as product details and movements, and will help you to keep track of what you have in stock, its financial value etc.

Additional product reports tailored to your business needs can be created using the Report Designer (See Chapter 12). To run a Product Report:

Use the Product Audit Trail to quickly track the movement of stock.

If you selected to print the report, the Windows Print dialog box appears. Use this to select which pages to print and to change your printer settings if necessary.

You can easily generate labels for your products by clicking on the Labels button from the Products toolbar.

1 From the Products window click Reports to bring up the Product Reports list

2 Double-click on the required folder and select a report

3 Ensure Preview is selected

4 Click Generate Report here

5 Enter any required Criteria

6 Click OK to generate report

7 Click Print, then OK and Close

Invoices

This chapter shows you how to produce invoices and credit notes for your products and services. Customers, Products and Nominal Accounts are directly linked to Invoicing so the invoices produced automatically update the relevant ledgers. Any raised invoices not posted or printed can be monitored. Quotes and Proformas can also be generated.

Covers

Chapter Seven

The Invoicing Toolbar

This toolbar provides facilities for generating invoices, quotes, proformas and credit notes for the goods you sell and the services you provide. Ledgers can be automatically updated, transactions printed out and reports generated for analysis.

New/Edit

To Create or View an Invoice, a Pro-forma or a Credit Note

Recurring

To Open Saved Skeleton or Recurring Transactions

Print

To Print an Invoice or a Credit Note

Update

To Update Ledgers

Labels

To Print Invoice Labels

Reports

To Run Invoicing Reports

Invoicing

Processing manually generated invoices, or batch invoicing, i.e. items not generated using Sage Line 50, has already been referred to in Chapters 2 and 3. Briefly, Chapter 2 (Customers) explains how to log invoices and credit notes within the system after they have been produced and sent to customers. Chapter 3 (Suppliers) explains how to record the invoices and credit notes you receive from your suppliers.

Invoicing deals with Sage Line 50 generated invoices, of which there are two basic types. Firstly there is the Product Invoice, which is used for invoicing customers for the products you sell. Each line of the invoice can be used for recording specific product items. Early discount settlement can be offered on these invoices and carriage charges applied.

Meanwhile, the Service Invoice is used to invoice customers you have provided a service for. An unlimited amount of text can be entered into the invoice describing the services supplied. Discount settlement can be applied and carriage charges recorded.

As Sage Line 50 generates these invoices, all the relevant details are automatically recorded and posted for you when you are ready. For invoices where the same information is entered regularly, the Memorise option saves the invoice as a template. This template can then be recalled when required and updated with the new information, saving valuable time.

Within Invoicing is the facility to generate credit notes for your customers, where products or services for example, have not been received or had to be returned. When these transactions are posted, the ledgers will be updated automatically.

You do, of course, need to keep track of your invoicing. Use the report facility regularly to print out a list of Invoices not yet printed or posted, or to check on stock requirements or shortfalls for the invoices you have generated using this Invoicing option.

In older versions of Sage Line 50, the Invoicing toolbar contained separate buttons for Product and Service Invoices and Credit Notes. With versions 10, 11 & 12, the toolbar contains only one New/Edit button. The type of Invoice or Credit Note is then selected from the Type and Format boxes in the Invoice window.

The Product Invoice

To invoice your customers for the products you sell, use the New/Edit option from the Invoicing toolbar, then select the Product option in the drop down list in the Type box. To create an Invoice click Modules, then Invoicing, from the menu bar and do the following:

You cannot amend a product invoice where the quantity was entered using the Sales Order Processing option.

1 Click New/Edit on the Invoicing toolbar. Invoice and Product appears here

3 Type Sales Order No. if applicable

2 Enter the tax point date if different here

4 Enter Customer Account Code

Provided the appropriate cost details have been entered on the Product records, use the Profit button to quickly calculate how much profit an Invoice makes.

As well as normal product codes, you can also enter special non-product codes:

S1 = *Special product item with price and VAT amount*

S2 = *Special product item, exempt for VAT (Tax code T0)*

S3 = *Special service item with price and VAT amount*

M = *Message, with a description and up to two comment lines*

5 Customer details appear here

6 Enter the Product Code here (use Finder button)

7 Enter Quantity

8 Repeat Steps 6 & 7 for further products, then click Save to finish

9 Click Close

Any changes made to the delivery details are not saved back to the Customer Record.

For a payment which has already been received and can be allocated against a product invoice, record it using the Payment Details tab.

Product Invoice Order Details

You can also record useful additional Order Details on your Invoice if necessary:

1 Click on Order Details tab

2 Enter Delivery Address

3 Enter any Notes if required

4 Enter Customer Order Details, especially Order No

Product Invoice Footer Details

Further details, such as Carriage and Settlement Terms, go in the Footer Details:

5 Click on Footer Details tab

6 Enter any Carriage details here

Using the Footer Details tab you can enter or amend any settlement terms, and add any analysis conditions that you wish to apply to the entire invoice, e.g. the Tax Code, Nominal Account Code and Department.

7 Record Settlement Terms here

8 Enter any Global detail changes

9 Click Save

10 Click Close to finish

Printing an Invoice

When using the Invoicing option to create invoices and credit notes, you can choose either to print straight away or save them as a batch for printing later using the Print option on the Invoicing Toolbar.

Sage Line 50 gives you the option to print Invoices or Credit Notes either immediately, or at a later date. To print straight away after you have entered all of the details, instead of clicking Save (the Invoice is automatically saved for you) do the following:

1 Click Print

2 Select a suitable file layout

Batching invoices or credit notes is useful if you only have one printer. Simply load the correct stationery in the printer, then print them all in one go.

3 Select Printer here

5 Click OK to print

If no records are selected from the list in the Invoicing window, all non-printed invoices or credit notes will be printed.

4 Click Generate Report

6 Select Preview then click OK

7 Click Close to finish

The Service Invoice

To avoid having to re-create the same invoice details all the time, store a template using the Memorise button or simply select the required item in the invoicing window and click Duplicate.

To invoice customers for the services you provide instead of products you sell, you should generate a Service Invoice, still using the New/Edit button from the Invoicing Toolbar. An unlimited amount of text can be entered to describe the services provided, and each service can be analysed to a different nominal account. Settlement discounts can also be applied as well as recording carriage charges.

As with Product Invoices, a Service Invoice can be saved to print in a batch later or printed straight away. At this point you have the option to update the ledgers at the same time or leave them until a more appropriate time.

Sage Line 50 warns you if a selected customer account has been marked as 'on hold' on the Customer Record.

1 Click New/Edit from the Invoicing toolbar and select Service here

2 Change date if different

3 Enter Order Number

4 Enter Customer Code

Select a service item and click on the Edit box or Press F3 to view item details. If required, you can alter the Posting Details or enter a Job Reference.

5 Type service Details here

6 Enter Net Price

7 Repeat Steps 5 & 6 as required

8 Click Save to print later, or Print to print now

9 Click Close to finish

Service Invoice Order Details

You can record useful additional Order Details on your Service Invoice if required:

If you make a mistake, simply click Discard and start again.

1 Click on Order Details tab

2 Enter Delivery Address

3 Enter any Notes if required

4 Enter Customer Order Details, especially Order No

Any changes made to the delivery details are not saved back to the Customer Record.

Service Invoice Footer Details

You can record details such as Carriage and Settlement Terms in the Footer Details box:

5 Click on Footer Details tab

6 Enter any Carriage details here

For payments you have received which can be allocated against the invoice, record the details using the Payment Details tab.

7 Record Settlement Terms here

8 Enter any Global detail changes

9 Click Save

10 Click Close to finish

The Skeleton Invoice

To bring up a list of all the invoices or orders that you have currently saved as skeletons or recurring transactions, click the Recurring button from the Invoice toolbar.

For information that is regularly repeated when creating an invoice, use the Memorise option to store the invoice as a template. You can then recall this template as and when required, and update it with the new information, thus saving valuable time and reduce keying errors.

This facility is available for both Product and Service Invoices, as well as the Product and Service Credit Notes.

1   On the Details screen enter regularly used details only, such as Customer A/C Ref. and item Details. Omit the Price

A quick way to alter the date in a Date box is to use the up or down cursor keys to move through the days. Pressing Page Up or Page Down moves through the months.

To have Line 50 Automatically generate this transaction for you at set regular intervals, just fill in the details and frequency here.

2   Click Memorise

3   Enter Filename and Description

4   Click Save

5   When you need to use a layout, click Recall

6   Select your layout from the list

7   Click Load

Product Credit Note

From time to time goods sent to customers may be returned as faulty, past an expiry date, etc, or the customer may simply have been overcharged by mistake.

A VAT only credit note can be raised where a customer has been invoiced and charged tax for goods which are exempt from VAT.

Instead of correcting the original invoice, a Product Credit Note can be issued to the Customer, detailing the amount owing to them. When your ledgers are updated, the necessary postings will be made to reflect this amendment. Do the following to create a Product Credit Note:

1 Click New/Edit from the Invoicing toolbar and select Credit here

2 Change date if different

3 Enter Order Number

4 Enter Customer Code

In Sage Line 50 you must always select the Invoice Format, i.e., Product or Service, prior to entering any product or service details. Once you begin to enter these details, the Format box goes to grey and can only be changed by discarding the Invoice and starting again.

5 When Customer is selected, details appear here

6 Enter the Product Code

7 Enter Quantity

8 Repeat Steps 6 & 7 as required, then click Save to finish

9 Click Close

Processing Recurring Transactions

You can turn off the recurring transaction reminder by selecting the No Recurring Entries at Startup check box in the Bank Defaults window from the Settings menu.

Information that is regularly repeated when creating a Product or Service Invoice or Credit note can be stored and later recalled for use as required or for updating. This feature is particulary useful for any recurring transactions you may have.

If the Frequency details were entered when the recurring transaction skeleton was created and memorised, Sage Line 50 will remind you automatically on startup if you have any outstanding transactions for processing. You can then choose to immediately post the transactions or process them at a later date as follows:

1 Click Recurring from the Invoicing toolbar to bring up the Memorised Invoices window

Processing recurring transactions is only available in Accountant Plus or Financial Controller.

2 Click Process

3 Remove tick here if entry is not to be processed, then No to process later

4 Click Process to produce your recurring transactions

5 Click Ok, then Cancel to close the memorised Invoices windows

When a recurring transaction is processed, only the invoice, purchase order or sales order is produced. You must then remember to post these items manually in order to update the ledgers or allocate any stock.

Updating your Ledgers

After creating your invoices and credit notes, the Update function is used to transfer details to the customer and nominal ledgers and, if appropriate, to amend product records.

By regularly updating your stock records, you may find you now have enough free stock to complete outstanding sales orders.

Sage Line 50 gives you the option to print the update report immediately, preview it first so that you can select only certain pages for printing, or to save the report as a file. To perform an Update, do the following:

1 From the Invoicing window select invoices/credit notes for updating

2 Click Update to display Output options

Always make sure you select at least one Invoice or Credit Note before using the Update function, otherwise Sage Line 50 will ask you if you want to process ALL non-posted invoices and credit notes.

3 In the Output box click Preview

4 Click OK to generate the update

6 Click Close to return to the Invoicing window, then Close again

5 On the report, click Print to bring up the Print dialog box, then click OK to print

Printing for Batch Invoicing

When you created Invoices or Credit Notes, for both Product or Service, you may have decided to leave printing them until later as a batch. This can often save time when setting up file layouts and having to change the printer stationery.

You can reprint your invoices as many times as you wish.

For example, you may have created two Service invoices which now need printing. You would do the following:

I — From the Invoicing window, select the invoices for printing

2 — Click Print

Use the Search button if you wish to print a number of invoices or credit notes that match a particular condition.

3 — Select Layout required

4 — Ensure Preview is selected

5 — Click on Generate Report

Standard layouts can always be edited or new layouts created as necessary.

6 — On the preview, click Print to bring up the Windows Print dialog box, then click OK to print

7 — Click Close to return to the Invoicing window

Producing Reports

The Reports option allows you to produce a wide range of reports about your product and service invoices, as well as your credit notes. Use these reports regularly to keep your business up to date. To print an invoice report:

Save time: instead of searching through all your invoices for those not yet posted, use the Invoices Not Posted report instead.

1 Click Reports from the Invoicing toolbar

2 Double-click on folder and select report required

3 Ensure Preview is selected

4 Click Generate Report to produce report

Use the Labels button from the Invoicing toolbar to quickly print out invoice address labels.

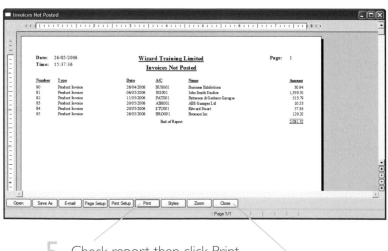

5 Check report then click Print

6 Click OK to print report

7 Click Close to finish

Processing Sales Orders

This chapter shows you how to keep track of your Sales Orders. You will learn how to allocate and despatch stock to these orders to keep your stock levels up-to-date. You will be shown how to automatically generate a Sales Invoice for each despatch you make and how to print Sales Orders, Delivery Notes and a variety of reports.

Covers

Chapter Eight

The Sales Order Processing Toolbar

The SOP toolbar provides a number of features for creating a sales order and then controlling the allocation of stock to that order. Once you are ready to deliver the stock, you can despatch it and Sage Line 50 will automatically handle the stock record updates. From this toolbar you can also print sales orders, whilst information regarding sales order processing can be easily obtained by using the various report layouts already provided for you.

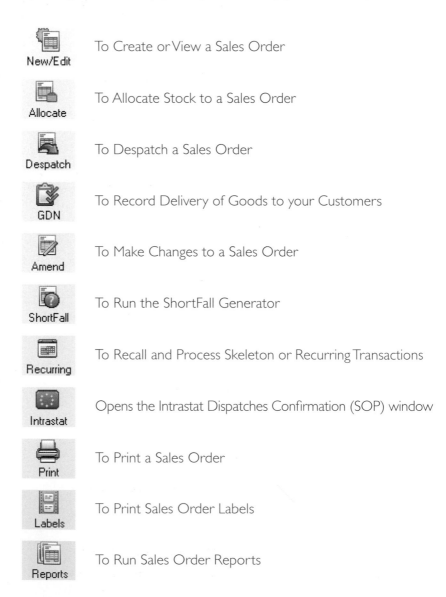

New/Edit — To Create or View a Sales Order

Allocate — To Allocate Stock to a Sales Order

Despatch — To Despatch a Sales Order

GDN — To Record Delivery of Goods to your Customers

Amend — To Make Changes to a Sales Order

ShortFall — To Run the ShortFall Generator

Recurring — To Recall and Process Skeleton or Recurring Transactions

Intrastat — Opens the Intrastat Dispatches Confirmation (SOP) window

Print — To Print a Sales Order

Labels — To Print Sales Order Labels

Reports — To Run Sales Order Reports

The Sales Order

Sales orders can be created for the products you supply and sent to customers by using the Enter option from the Sales Order Processing toolbar. Details from your Product records are automatically entered onto the Sales Orders whilst extra details can also be added, such as a delivery address, a customer order number for future reference or a settlement discount.

To create a Sales Order, click Modules, Sales Order Processing from the Sage Line 50 menu bar, then do the following:

1 Click New/Edit from the Sales Order Processing toolbar

2 Type required date if different to current date

4 Customer details appear here

3 Enter Customer Account Code

5 Enter the Product Code here (use Finder button)

6 Enter Quantity ordered here

7 Repeat Steps 5 & 6 for additional products, then if finished click Save

8 Click Close

...cont'd

Sales Order Details

On the previous page you were shown how to create a Sales Order and save it immediately if no further details need to be entered. Sage Line 50, however, gives you the option to enter additional details about the order, such as where it should be delivered if different from the main address.

From the Sales Order window, do the following to enter additional order details:

Once a Sales Order has been despatched in part or full, you cannot decrease the quantity of a product to less than the quantity despatched.

1 Click on the Order Details tab

2 Enter Delivery Address (not yet set up) if required

3 Record any Notes here

Sage Line 50 will generate an invoice and enter the Invoice Number automatically for you when the order is Despatched.

If you trade physical goods with Member States of the EU, use the Intrastat button for producing trade statistics. The supply of services is excluded. Intrastat replaced customs declarations as the source of trade statistics within the EU and is closely linked with the VAT system. Use F1 Help key for more information.

4 Enter any relevant Customer Order Details, such as a Customer Order Number

5 You may wish to enter Due Despatch date here

6 Click Save when finished

7 Click Close

Allocating Stock

To view Sales Order details simply double-click on the item.

Once a Sales Order has been created, stock needs allocating to it before any despatches can be recorded for the Order. Using the Allocate option from the Sales Order Processing toolbar automatically allocates the necessary stock needed for the selected Sales Order.

If Sage Line 50 cannot allocate all of the necessary stock to the order, a message box is displayed, giving suggestions and possible reasons why not.

Sometimes there is insufficient stock available to complete an Order, in which case the Order will be marked as 'Part' complete. There may be times when you have enough stock, but wish to only send part of the Order. In this case you would use the Amend option to make changes to the Order. To allocate batched Sales Orders, do the following from within the Sales Order Processing window:

| Click on the Sales Orders you wish to Allocate

2 Click Allocate

If there is insufficient stock for a Sales Order, the Status 'Part' appears in the Sales Order Processing window. Fully allocated orders display 'Full'.

3 Click Yes to Confirm Allocation of stock

4 Note change in Sales Order Status

5 Click Close

Despatching Sales Orders

If only part of an order is despatched, Sage Line 50 creates an invoice for that part. This means that when the order is fully despatched, there will be more than one invoice for it.

Once stock is allocated to your sales orders, it can be despatched at any time. The Despatch option also updates the product records and creates a Product Invoice for the order, as well as printing a Delivery Note.

The product invoices created through Sales Order Processing appears in the Invoicing window. These invoices can be edited, but you cannot change the quantity of the product despatched. They can then be printed and posted to the sales and nominal ledgers in the same manner as invoices created using the Invoicing option.

Click the Complete button from the Sales Order window to automatically save the order, Allocate stock to it and record the Despatch all in one go.

1 From the Sales Order Processing window, select the required Sales Orders

2 Click Despatch

3 Click Yes to print Delivery Notes, if required, create Invoices and Update Stock

Use the Shortfall option to see if you have enough stock to fulfil orders or to place purchase orders if you do not.

5 Select Delivery Note layout

6 Click Generate Report

4 Click here to confirm you want to print the Delivery Notes now

You can use the GDN button from the toolbar to quickly generate a Goods Delivery Note. Remember, though, that if you set up your GDN Options to 'Do not Generate', Line 50 will not produce a goods despatch note and the GDN option does not appear on the SOP toolbar.

7 Print required Delivery Notes, then Close all windows

Amending & Printing Sales Orders

When you Amend the allocation of stock to a sales order, the allocated status of the order in the Sales Orders window may change to either Full, Part or no status at all.

If you have allocated stock to a sales order, but have not yet despatched all of it, you can amend this allocation. This allows you to despatch a full order by reducing the stock allocation of another customer's order, hence perhaps reducing the number of customers waiting.

To amend the allocation of stock on a sales order

Remember that you can raise an invoice even if you have a negative stock situation.

1 Select the Order from the Sales Order Processing window and click Amend

2 Amend the Allocation

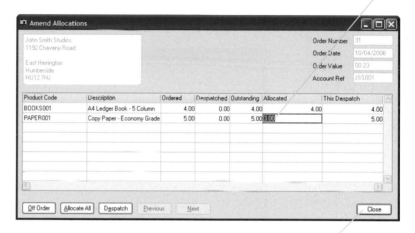

3 Click Close and note any change in Status

Printing Batched Orders

By batching your orders, you can print them all out together after setting up the printer with the correct sales order stationery.

1 Select orders for printing from Sales Order Processing window and Click Print

2 Select layout required

3 Click Generate Report

4 Click Print, then Close

Sales Orders Reports

Sage Line 50 provides you with a large variety of reports to help you run the Sales Order side of your business. For example, you have the facility to print a picking list for your warehouse from a particular order or the sales order shortage report to show you any shortfalls in the stock.

These reports are generated from the information entered when you created a sales order. To generate, for example, a Sales Order Picking List:

1 From the Sales Order Processing window, click Reports

2 Double-click appropriate folder & select required Layout

3 Check Output is set to Preview

4 Click here to view report

5 Enter Criteria i.e. Sales Order number

6 Click OK to generate report

7 Click Print to send to printer, then OK & Close

Purchase Orders

In this chapter you will learn how to create and print Purchase Orders to send to your suppliers. You will be shown how to monitor orders raised and record deliveries received as well as produce reports to help you keep track of your Purchase Orders.

Covers

Chapter Nine

Purchase Order Processing Toolbar

From the POP toolbar you can create and print Purchase Orders as well as make amendments to orders you have already created. You have facilities for recording deliveries and producing useful reports about your Purchase Orders, such as a report indicating orders that have been delivered in part or full, or orders that are still outstanding.

 New/Edit — To Create or View a Purchase Order

Order — To Put a Purchase Order 'on order'

Deliver — To Record Purchase Order Deliveries

GRN — To Complete a Goods Received Note

Amend — To Make Changes to a Purchase Order

Update — To Automatically Update the Purchase Ledger

Recurring — To Recall and Process Skeleton or Recurring Transactions

Intrastat — Opens the Intrastat Arrivals Confirmation (POP) window

Print — To Print a Purchase Order

Labels — To Print Purchase Order Labels

Reports — To Run Purchase Order Reports

Creating a Purchase Order

To edit an existing purchase order simply double-click on it in the Purchase Order Processing window.

To record order details of any products you buy from a supplier, use the Enter option from the Purchase Order toolbar. Details entered straight onto the Purchase Order screen are taken directly from the product records for you by Sage Line 50.

You can also include additional details, such as delivery address or any settlement discount given to you by your supplier, to the order. To create a Purchase Order click POP from the Sage Line 50 toolbar then follow these steps:

1 Click New/Edit from the Purchase Orders Processing toolbar

2 Check required date is entered here

You can increase, but not decrease, the quantity for any Purchase Order you have already despatched in full or part.

4 Supplier details appear here

3 Enter Supplier Account Code

For non-payment products use the product code M.

5 Enter the Product Code here (use Finder button)

6 Enter Quantity being ordered

7 Repeat Steps 5 & 6 for additional products, click Save when finished

8 Click Close

Entering Purchase Order Details

You may need to record further details on your Purchase Order, such as delivery details, carriage costs, settlement terms, supplier contact or the name of the person who took your order.

Sage Line 50 lets you do this through the Order Details or Footer Details tabs. From the Purchase Order window, do the following to enter additional order details:

Save your Purchase Order as a Skeleton if you use these details regularly.

1 Click on the Order Details tab

2 Enter Delivery Address here if required

3 Record any Notes you wish to add here

Use the Footer Details tab to record any Carriage or Settlement terms and the Deliveries tab to view delivery information.

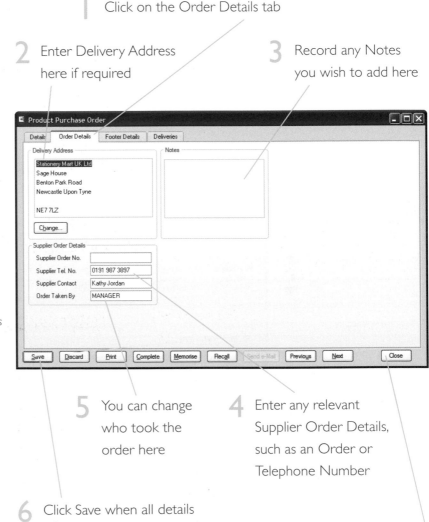

5 You can change who took the order here

4 Enter any relevant Supplier Order Details, such as an Order or Telephone Number

6 Click Save when all details have been entered.

7 Click Close

Placing Purchase Orders 'on order'

Once a Purchase Order has been created, it has to be placed 'on order' before any deliveries can be recorded for it. The Sage Line 50 program then updates each product record with the new order details accordingly.

Click the Search button to set up a filter to list only the orders you wish to work with.

Use the Order option to automatically place a single or batch of Purchase Orders 'on order', as follows:

1 From the Purchase Order Processing window, highlight all the orders you wish to place 'on order' by clicking on them

2 Click Order

To avoid costly mistakes, always check that the status of an order shows ON-ORDER after going through the process of placing it on order.

3 Click No here to print a copy of the Purchase Order later, else Yes to print now

You can also put Purchase Orders 'on order' from within the Amend Deliveries option.

4 Click Yes to Confirm you wish to place the selected items 'on order'

5 Note that items are now ON-ORDER

6 Click Close

Recording Deliveries

To automatically record the complete delivery of stock for Purchase Orders use the Deliver option from the Purchase Order Processing toolbar.

When you use the Delivery option it is assumed that you have taken full delivery of all items on the Purchase Order. The Delivery record cannot be altered later.

You should remember that Sage Line 50 always assumes that you have taken full delivery of all the products needed to complete the selected Purchase Order. If a part delivery needs recording, you must record the delivery using the Amend function (see page 116).

To record Purchase Order deliveries do the following:

1 From the Purchase Order Processing window select any orders you wish to mark as Delivered

You can only record deliveries for orders which you have already put 'on order'.

2 Click Deliver

4 Note the Purchase Order now displays as COMPLETE

Sage Line 50 automatically makes adjustments for each product that you mark as delivered.

3 Click Yes in this box to Confirm delivery and update stock records, then choose whether to print a GRN now or later

5 If finished, Click Close

Processing Purchases Manually

To check and keep track of your Purchase Orders use the Amend option. In this window you can manually place them 'on order' (thus updating On Order levels for the appropriate product records), record full or part deliveries of stock against each order and cancel orders.

You can cancel a Purchase Order which is 'on order' using the Amend option. Just click Off Order to mark it as cancelled, click Order to put it back 'on order'.

Placing a Purchase Order 'on order' manually

You have already learned how to place Purchase Orders 'on order' using the Order button (Page 113). However, Sage Line 50 also allows you to do this manually as follows:

1 From Purchase Order Processing window, select the purchase order you require

2 Click Amend to bring up the Amend Deliveries window

You can use the GRN button from the toolbar to quickly generate a Goods Received Note. Remember, though, that if you set up your GRN Options in Invoice and Order Defaults to 'Do not Generate', Line 50 will not produce a goods received note and the GRN option does not appear on the POP toolbar.

3 Click on the Order button to place 'on order'

4 Note the order now looks normal and the full order quantity appears in This Delivery

5 Click Close

Recording Deliveries Manually

You use the Deliver button from the Purchase Order Processing toolbar only when you have received full delivery of an order.

If you wish to record part deliveries, then you must use the Amend option, though you can still record full deliveries this way as well, should you need to. To record a Purchase Order part delivery, follow these steps:

If the order is not 'on order' or has been cancelled, Line 50 reminds you to place the Purchase Order 'on order' to enable you to record the delivery.

1 From the Purchase Order Processing window select the order you wish to record a delivery for

2 Click Amend

Use the GRN button from the Purchase Order Processing toolbar to quickly produce Goods Received Notes.

4 Click on the Deliver button to update your product record details

3 Enter the part quantity received in the This Delivery column

Use the Amend option if you wish to record part deliveries for your Purchase Orders.

5 Click Yes to confirm updating of order

6 Click Close to finish & note status is PART

Printing Batched Purchase Orders

Why not save time by emailing your Purchase Orders directly to your Suppliers.

Rather than print your Purchase Orders straight away you may have chosen to save them until later. This is useful if you only have one printer and need to change the stationery. When you are ready you can then print the orders out in batches.

As with all the printing facilities in Sage Line 50, you can send the Purchase Order direct to the printer, save it as a file or first preview it on the screen. To preview an order and then print it do the following:

1 From the Purchase Order Processing window, select the order for printing

2 Click Print

To print a specific selection of Purchase Orders use the Search button facility.

3 Select correct layout

4 Ensure Preview is selected

5 Click Generate Report

If your business trades physical goods with Member States of the EU, use the Intrastat button for producing trade statistics.

6 On the preview, click Print to bring up the Print dialog box, then click OK

7 Click Close

9. Purchase Orders **117**

Purchase Order Reports

Standard reports have already been set up for you to display any outstanding Purchase Orders, or orders which have already been delivered or part delivered. These reports can be previewed on screen, sent to your printer or saved to a file for previewing or printing later.

To generate a report of any Purchase Orders not yet delivered, do the following:

1 From the Purchase Order Processing toolbar, click Reports

Use the Purchase Order Not Delivered or Part Delivered report to track and monitor your supplies.

2 Select required layout

3 Check Preview is selected

4 Click on Generate Report

5 Enter Criteria, if any applies

6 Click OK to generate report

Use the Outstanding Purchase Orders report regularly to help you keep track of orders still outstanding for delivery.

7 Click Print to send to printer, then OK & Close

Financials

This chapter shows you how to generate a variety of financial reports so you can analyse your business transactions. This includes the Trial Balance, Profit & Loss, the Balance Sheet, the Budget and Prior Year reports. You will learn how to produce an automated VAT Return as well as a detailed Audit Trail, which lists every transaction recorded within the system.

Covers

Chapter Ten

The Financials Toolbar

From this toolbar you can generate all the financial reports you need to not only keep track of how your business is doing financially but also trace back and find out when certain transactions took place. The Audit Trail is particularly useful as it is a complete record of your transaction activities, whilst the VAT function gives you all the features you need to produce accurate VAT Returns.

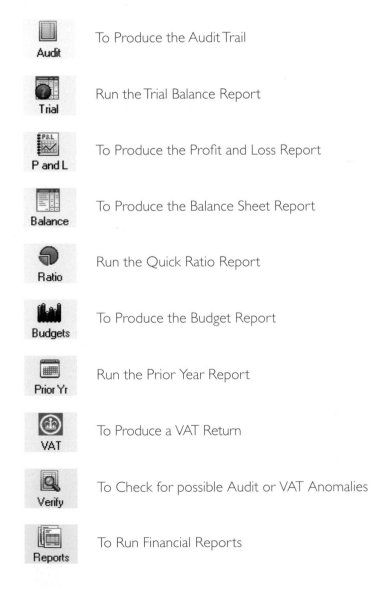

Audit — To Produce the Audit Trail

Trial — Run the Trial Balance Report

P and L — To Produce the Profit and Loss Report

Balance — To Produce the Balance Sheet Report

Ratio — Run the Quick Ratio Report

Budgets — To Produce the Budget Report

Prior Yr — Run the Prior Year Report

VAT — To Produce a VAT Return

Verify — To Check for possible Audit or VAT Anomalies

Reports — To Run Financial Reports

The Audit Trail

Deleted transactions always appear in red.

The Audit Trail records details about transactions entered into the system and it is a very useful source of information for checking and cross referencing. It may also be referred to when auditing your accounts.

Sage Line 50 gives you a range of Audit Trail formats providing brief, summary or fully detailed reports which can be previewed, printed directly or saved as a file for use later. A report of deleted transactions can also be printed. Use the Audit Trail regularly to ensure your transactions are being recorded accurately. To view the Audit Trail:

Transaction codes used in the Audit Trail are explained on Page 49.

1 From the Sage Line 50 menu bar, click Modules then Financials to bring up the Financials window displaying the Audit Trail

No	Type	Account	Nominal	Dept	Details	Date	Ref	Ex.Ref	Net	Tax
1503	PI	CON001	5000	2	Rubber Bands - Selection Pack (200)	03/05/2006	33		648.00	
1504	PI	CON001	5000	2	A4 Ledger Book - 5 Column	03/05/2006	33		450.00	
1505	PI	CON001	5000	2	A4 Carbon Copy Book - Triplicate	03/05/2006	33		738.00	
1506	PI	CON001	5000	2	Pencil - Chinagraph Black	03/05/2006	33		198.00	
1507	PI	CON001	5000	2	Calculator - Printing Rolls	03/05/2006	33		549.00	
1508	PI	CON001	5000	2	Ball Point Pen - Black	03/05/2006	33		540.00	
1509	PI	CON001	5000	2	Ball Point Pen - Blue	03/05/2006	33		720.00	
1510	PC	MCN001	5001	2	Cancel - see tran 1150	27/04/2004	Cancel		1620.00	
1511	PI	MCN001	5001	2	MTH1000 Motherboard	27/05/2006	34		270.00	
1512	PI	MCN001	5001	2	MTH2000 Motherboard	27/05/2006	34		360.00	
1513	PI	MCN001	5001	2	DIMM 64mb 100Mhz	27/05/2006	34		387.00	
1514	PI	MCN001	5001	2	10gb Hard Drive	27/05/2006	34		288.00	
1515	PI	MCN001	5001	2	30gb Hard Drive	27/05/2006	34		648.00	
1516	PI	MCN001	5001	2	MTH3000 Motherboard	27/05/2006	34		450.00	
1517	PI	MCN001	5001	2	DIMM 128mb 100Mhz	27/05/2006	34		738.00	
1518	PI	MCN001	5001	2	DIMM 32mb 100Mhz	27/05/2006	34		198.00	
1519	PI	MCN001	5001	2	SIMM 64mb 100Mhz	27/05/2006	34		549.00	
1520	PI	MCN001	5001	2	15" Monitor	27/05/2006	34		540.00	
1521	PI	MCN001	5001	2	17" Monitor	27/05/2006	34		720.00	
1522	PI	MCN001	5001	2	19" Monitor	27/05/2006	34		1620.00	

When you clear transactions from the Audit Trail, Sage Line 50 brings them forward as opening balances in your financial reports.

2 Use both horizontal and vertical arrow buttons and scroll bars to examine all transaction details

3 When you have finished examining the Audit Trail, click Close

To print the Audit Trail report

The Criteria box options vary according to the type of Audit Trail report selected.

1 From the Financials toolbar click Audit

2 Select Audit Trail Type required, i.e. Brief

3 Check Output is set to Preview

4 Click Run to continue

5 Enter required Criteria

6 Click here to Exclude Deleted Transactions from the report

You can choose to exclude deleted transactions from your reports and instead, print them as a separate report later.

7 Click OK to Continue

8 If you want to print the report, click Print, then OK

Make sure you print your Audit Trail reports at least every month to use for reference purposes.

9 Close the window

The Trial Balance

You can run this report for any month as it proves a valuable source for management information.

This report displays a simple listing of current balances in all your nominal ledger accounts. It shows total values for both the debit and credit entries for all the nominal codes containing a balance value.

Since Sage Line 50 controls the double-entry accounting for you, the debit and credit columns will always balance. To produce the Trial Balance report do the following:

1 From the Financials toolbar click Trial. This brings up the Print Output window

2 Ensure Preview is selected

3 Click Run

4 Click here and select period required. Scroll down if necessary

5 Click OK to generate the Trial Balance

When you open the Financials window, the display automatically jumps down to the bottom of the list so the most recently entered transactions are displayed.

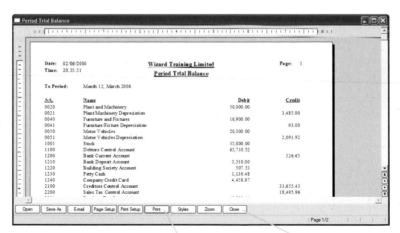

6 To print, click Print, then OK

7 Click Close

Profit and Loss Report

Balances are posted before the start of the financial year and so will appear as a prior year adjustment on the balance sheet, not on the Profit and Loss Report.

This important financial report shows whether your business is trading at a profit over a particular period of time. The report can be produced for the current month or a range of consecutive months within your current financial year.

The balances of each of your income and expenditure nominal ledger accounts appear on the standard Profit and Loss report. These categories, i.e. Sales, Purchases, Direct Expenses and Overheads, are grouped together and display a sub-total. The Gross Profit/(Loss) and Net Profit/(Loss) amount is also shown.

1 From the Financials window click P and L

2 Ensure Preview is selected

3 Click Run

4 Enter the From and To Period required

5 Select Default Layout of Accounts (1)

6 Click OK

Unless you have set up your own layout, ensure you choose the Default Layout of Accounts in Step 3, otherwise you will not generate the correct report.

7 To print, click Print, then OK

8 Click Close

The Balance Sheet

Use the Balance Sheet regularly to give a summary of your current financial position.

The Balance Sheet shows the financial position of a business at a particular time by outlining its assets (what it owns) and its liabilities (what it owes). There are two main types of assets, fixed and current. Fixed assets are long-term and have material substance such as, premises, equipment and vehicles; whilst current assets are continually changing and include stock, debtors, cash accounts, etc.

The Balance Sheet shows the fixed and current assets, as well as the liabilities. By adding together the assets and subtracting the liabilities, the Balance Sheet shows the Capital, or net assets.

The difference between assets and liabilities is referred to as the company's net assets (or net worth).

1 Click Balance from the Financials toolbar

2 Ensure Preview is selected

3 Click Run

4 Enter the From and To Period required

5 Select Default Layout of Accounts (1)

6 Click OK

Liabilities consist of both current and long-term. Current liabilities are amounts owing at the balance sheet date and due for repayment within 12 months or less, e.g. trade creditors. Long-term liabilities are amounts due for repayment in more than 12 months, e.g. bank loan.

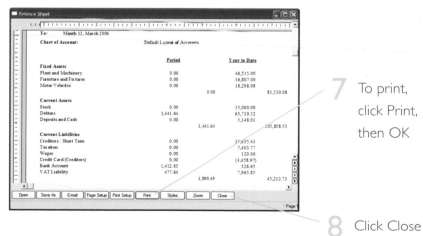

7 To print, click Print, then OK

8 Click Close

Quick Ratio Report

Use the Quick Ratio Report to see the immediate financial position of your company. This is useful when you are considering future investments etc.

Using the data available within the system, the Quick Ratio Report allows you to see the current liquidity position of the business. This type of information is necessary for making financial decisions about future investments or developments and will be required by a number of different parties, for example: management, bank managers, shareholders.

These Ratio Reports highlight both the strengths and the weaknesses in the financial position of your business. Credit and debit balances are compared to show the net balance using previously set up nominal account codes. You can edit the report to include other nominal accounts you wish to compare.

To view or edit the quick ratio report

1 From the Financials window, click Ratio

2 To edit the nominal accounts, use Finder button to select Nominal Code required

Click the Save button to quickly store a Quick Ratio report for future reference.

N/C Ref	N/C Name	Debit	Credit
1100	Debtors Control Account	74035.45	0.00
1103	Prepayments	0.00	0.00
1200	Bank Current Account	0.00	1477.39
1210	Bank Deposit Account	3510.00	0.00
1220	Building Society Account	507.53	0.00
1230	Petty Cash	1130.48	0.00
1240	Company Credit Card	4458.97	0.00
2100	Creditors Control Account	0.00	44018.46
2109	Accruals	0.00	0.00
2200	Sales Tax Control Accour	0.00	19735.84
2201	Purchase Tax Control Acc	12083.73	0.00
3200	Profit and Loss Account	0.00	0.00
4000	Sales North	0.00	173686.67

142987.19

3 Click Print, then Run in Print Output window

4 Select Period

5 Click OK

The Budget Report

You can amend your nominal account Budget values at any time by using the Global Changes feature from the Tools menu.

The Budget Report displays the current values in your purchases, sales, direct expenses and overhead account codes for the months you select and the year-to-date. Use this report to see how your business actually traded compared with the monthly budget you set against the nominal ledger accounts for the chosen months and the year-to-date.

1 Click Budgets from the Financials toolbar

2 Ensure Preview is selected & click Run

3 In the Criteria box enter the From and To Period required

4 Select Default Layout of Accounts (1)

5 Click OK to generate the report

When you run a year end, Sage Line 50 offers you the option to move the actual monthly values for the year just ended to the budgets for the coming year. This sets the budget values to be what really happened in each month of the year just ended. You can also add a percentage increase to your budget values to reflect any anticipated rise in sales, purchases, costs, etc. for the coming year.

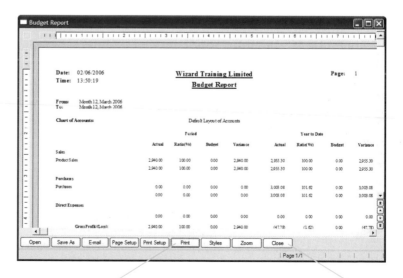

6 To print, click Print, then OK

7 Click Close

The Prior Year Report

The Prior Year Report compares the current values in your purchases, sales, direct expenses and overhead accounts codes using the formats as set up for you in your chart of accounts. Trading activities are detailed for both the current month and the year-to-date, or alternatively for any period you specify.

This report compares how your business is trading for the specified period against the same period in the previous year. Year-to-date totals and ratios are also included. To produce a Prior Year report do the following:

1 Click Prior Yr from the Financials toolbar

You can create your own specific report layouts for different Chart of Accounts.

2 Ensure Preview is selected & click Run

3 In the Criteria box enter the From and To Period required

5 Click OK to generate the report

4 Select Default Layout of Accounts (1)

If you wish to create a new Chart of Accounts layout simply refer to Page 55.

6 To print, click Print, then OK

7 Click Close

The VAT Return

Use the Wizard button to guide you through the stages of the VAT Return process.

For businesses that need to submit VAT Return forms to HM Customs & Excise, or HM Revenue and Customs as it is now known, Sage Line 50 provides all the features to enable you to do this quickly and accurately, calculating both input and output tax for you from the information you have entered over the period. This is a prime reason for keeping accurate accounts.

Input tax is the VAT you are charged on your business purchases and expenses. Output tax is the VAT your business charges on its taxable supplies or services. Since Value Added Tax is a tax charged to the final consumer, a business needs to calculate what input tax can be reclaimed and how much output tax needs paying to Revenue and Customs. This is the purpose of the VAT Return.

Before reconciling your VAT transactions, you should back up your data files.

Reconciling your transactions sets a flag against each transaction so it is automatically excluded from subsequent VAT Returns.

You have the facility to set up 100 tax codes, but on installation Sage Line 50 sets the standard UK and EC VAT rates for you, so you will probably not have to change anything. The default is set to the standard rate T1, presently at 17.5%, whilst others you may need are T0 (zero-rated) and T9 (transactions not involving VAT).

Within the nominal ledger there are three accounts, namely Sales Tax Control account (2200), Purchase Tax Control account (2201) and VAT liability account (2202). An accumulated total appears in the Sales account for the output tax charged to your customers whilst another accumulated total appears in the Purchase account for the input tax charged to your business.

The Audit Trail VAT column shows whether a transaction is reconciled or not:

- *R = reconciled*

- *N = unreconciled*

- *a hyphen (-) or a dash (–) = a non-VAT transaction*

When your VAT Return is due, enter the correct date range into the system and the program will calculate the difference between the input and output tax and will inform you of the net VAT due to either the Revenue and Customs or to yourselves.

After reconciling your VAT Return, VAT on the Sales and Purchases Control accounts for this VAT period need to be transferred to the VAT Liability nominal account. When a bank payment to the Revenue and Customs is made or received, the VAT Liability account is cleared, leaving a zero balance.

...cont'd

Ensure all transactions have been reconciled and the Audit Trail checked before running your VAT Return.

Use the Verify button to quickly run a series of basic checks to highlight possible Audit or VAT anomalies before running the VAT Return.

Three reports are available for printing: Detailed, Summary and the VAT Return. The Detailed and Summary reports give a breakdown of all the totals from each box on the VAT Return.

To produce your VAT Return

1 From the Financials window click VAT to bring up the VAT Return window displaying zero totals

2 Enter the inclusive VAT period dates here

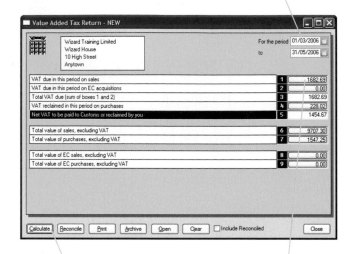

3 Click Calculate to calculate totals for this return. You will be informed if any unreconciled transactions have been found

4 Click on a VAT total for a breakdown

5 Double-click on a Tax Code for a transaction breakdown

6 Close each window to return to VAT Return

7 Click Print, Run and OK to print the return

8 Click Reconcile & confirm Yes

The VAT Transfer Wizard

Use the VAT Transfer Wizard to guide you through the transfer of your VAT liability once you have successfully reconciled and printed your VAT return.

Use the VAT Transfer Wizard to transfer money from the Sales and Purchase Tax Control accounts to the VAT Liability account.

1 From the Line 50 menu, click Modules, select Wizards, then click VAT Transfer Wizard

2 Click Yes to confirm you wish to continue

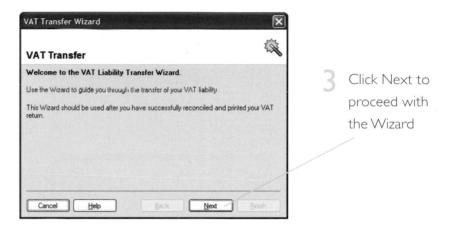

3 Click Next to proceed with the Wizard

Note that Sage Line 50 already has the following tax rates set up:

T0 = zero rated transactions

T1 = standard rate

T2 = exempt transactions

T4 = sales to customers in EC

T7 = zero rated purchases from suppliers in EC

T8 = standard rated purchases from suppliers in EC

T9 = transactions not involving VAT

4 Work your way through each screen entering details where required and clicking Next until you reach the Confirm Posting Details window

5 Click Finish to confirm details or Cancel to discard

Financial Reports

With Sage Line 50 you can calculate profit and loss for the current month or for any range of consecutive months within your current financial year.

Sage Line 50 offers a wide range of Financial Reports that provide management information to enable effective decision-making, planning and forecasting.

A considerable number of reports are set up at installation time, but many can be customised if required for your business by changing the appearance of the layout, the font type or by adding/removing certain text. Refer to Chapter 12 for more details. To generate a report do the following:

1 From the Financials toolbar click Reports

2 Double-click folder and select the report layout required

The grouping and positioning of nominal codes on the Financial Reports are determined by the relevant Chart of Account.

3 Check Output is set to Preview

4 Click Generate Report

5 Enter appropriate Criteria here

6 Click OK to generate the report, then Print

To Verify System

Information used for creating Financial Reports is taken from the actuals column in the Nominal Ledger Record.

1 Click Verify from Financials toolbar

2 Click OK to run checks

Fixed Assets

This chapter explains how to work with Fixed Asset Records and how to view the value of your assets by running Fixed Asset Reports. It also details the three accepted methods of depreciation offered by Sage Line 50, enabling you to decide which is the most appropriate method to use for your business.

Covers

Chapter Eleven

The Fixed Assets Toolbar

This toolbar features options for creating Fixed Asset Records and setting up the method of depreciation, performing valuation of Fixed Assets and the generation of your Fixed Asset reports.

To Create a Fixed Asset Record

To Report on Asset Valuation

To Dispose a Fixed Asset

To Run Fixed Asset Reports

Note:
In Sage Line 50 V12 there is no Fixed Assets button on the navigation bar. Instead, do the following to bring up the Fixed Assets window:

1   On the Sage Line 50 menu bar, click Modules

2   Click on Fixed Assets Register to bring up the Fixed Assets window

Recording your Fixed Assets

Have the following information ready before entering your Fixed Asset Records; purchase date of asset and cost price, depreciation method and rate, depreciation balance sheet nominal code and depreciation profit and loss nominal code.

Fixed Assets are items such as office equipment, buildings, machinery, etc. owned by the business. Their depreciation is an expense and can be offset against profits.

However, before recording Fixed Asset information, it is important that the correct method and rate of depreciation be decided upon and applied consistently. Different classes of Fixed Assets are often depreciated at different rates, for example, office furniture may be depreciated at a different rate to motor vehicles.

Sage Line 50 offers the choice of three depreciation methods: Straight Line, Reducing Balance and Write Off. For the Straight Line method, the asset is depreciated by a fixed percentage (calculated from the original Cost Price of the asset) every month until the asset is reduced to zero. For the Reducing Balance method, the asset is depreciated again monthly by a fixed percentage, but this time the percentage is applied to the new book value of the asset.

The last method, Write Off depreciation, makes one last posting to depreciate the remaining value of the asset.

When ready to enter your fixed assets for the first time you will notice that the Fixed Assets window is empty. As soon as Fixed Asset Records are entered, they will be displayed one record per line. To bring up the Fixed Assets window and view details:

To delete an Asset, simply highlight it in the Fixed Assets window, then click the Delete button.

1 From Modules, click Fixed Assets Register

2 Asset records appear here

3 Double-click on a record to view details

4 Click Close

You cannot save a new record unless the nominal ledger posting details have been entered.

Adding Fixed Asset Records

The first time you use the Assets option, the Fixed Assets window will be empty. To add a Fixed Asset record, have all the necessary information to hand, then do the following:

1 From the Fixed Assets toolbar click Record

2 Enter a unique code to easily identify asset, no spaces allowed

3 Type a Description here

Use the Tab key to move from one data entry box to the next.

4 Enter a Serial Number for extra information

5 Enter Location if relevant

6 Enter Date Purchased here

Fixed Asset Record

Details | Posting

Asset Reference	W12ARD ▾ New Asset
Description	BMW 320i M Sport
Serial Number	W12ARD
Location/Employee	Garage
Date Purchased	01/10/2005 Supplier A/C ▾
Assets	1 Directors Cars ▾

Save | Delete | Discard | Previous | Next | Close

7 If the asset was bought from one of your current Suppliers, select A/C here

8 For reporting purposes you can categorise your fixed assets. Select Asset Category from drop down list here

Although you have now entered all the relevant details for this asset, before you can save this new record you still need to enter the appropriate nominal ledger posting details. This is explained on the next two pages.

Fixed Asset Depreciation

The Fixed Asset option does not post depreciation for you, only records the asset and current value. Use Month End option to automatically make monthly depreciation postings.

The Posting Tab in Fixed Asset Record window is used for entering the necessary nominal ledger posting details. Then, when you run the Month End/Year End depreciation posting routines, asset depreciation will be added to the appropriate account code as an expense to your business and will be shown on the Balance Sheet & Profit and Loss Report.

There are four depreciation accounts already set up in the Balance Sheet of the nominal ledger by Sage Line 50. Every time an asset is depreciated, the amount of ` is posted as a credit posting. Codes include 0021 (Plant/Machinery Depreciation), 0031 (Office Equipment Depreciation), 0041 (Furniture/Fixture Depreciation) and 0051 (Motor Vehicles Depreciation).

Once you have saved a record, the depreciation method can only ever be changed to Write Off.

Similarly, four depreciation accounts are already set up for you in the Profit and Loss section of the nominal ledger. Every time an asset is depreciated, the value of that depreciation is added to the account code as an expense to the company (debit posting). Codes include 8001 (Plant/Machinery Depreciation), 8002 (Furniture/Fitting Depreciation), 8003 (Vehicle Depreciation) and 8004 (Office Equipment Depreciation).

You need to enter the annual rate of depreciation. For the Straight Line method, the value entered will be divided by twelve to calculate the monthly depreciation. For example, to depreciate an asset completely over five years using the straight line method, the Depreciation Rate would be 20%, depreciating at 1.666% monthly until after five years the book value is zero. So, for an item costing £15,000, a depreciation value of £250 would be posted for a term of 60 months.

To record a Fixed Asset Disposal simply click on the Disposal button on the Fixed Assets toolbar and follow the step-by-step Wizard.

Where Book Value details are required, then enter the current book value. If the asset is brand new, this should be the same as the Cost Price. If an asset has already been depreciated, then enter the cost price minus depreciation. If the reducing balance method was selected, the Book Value will be used to calculate the depreciation amount. Sage Line 50 will then automatically reduce this value by the depreciation amount when the month end procedure is run.

Depreciation and Valuation

Setting up a Fixed Asset depreciation posting

From the Fixed Assets window, click the Valuation button to quickly check the total cost, total current book value and the total amount of depreciation that has taken place so far on all of your asset records.

1 After entering the Fixed Asset Record details (page 136) select the Posting tab

2 Select Department where appropriate

3 Enter the nominal ledger balance sheet account code

4 Enter nominal ledger profit and loss account code

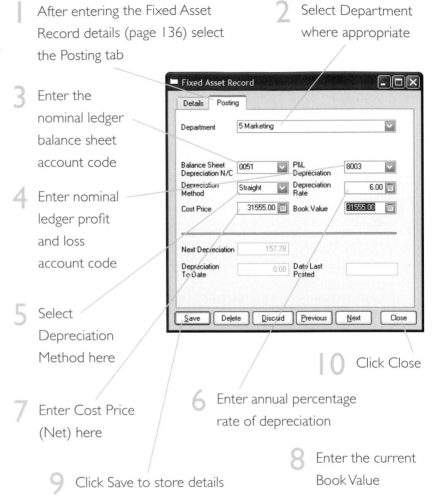

5 Select Depreciation Method here

You can save non-depreciating assets as well as depreciation assets.

7 Enter Cost Price (Net) here

6 Enter annual percentage rate of depreciation

10 Click Close

8 Enter the current Book Value

9 Click Save to store details

Valuation of Fixed Assets

To see details about the current value of your assets including total cost, previous total depreciation and total current book value do the following:

1 From the Fixed Assets window click Valuation to bring up the Asset Valuation window

2 When finished, click Close

The Report Designer

This chapter shows you how to create a new report and how to edit an existing report to meet your own requirements. Report Designer is very powerful and provides options for grouping and sorting information, adding calculations such as totals, setting up criteria and filters to search for information as well as designing the layout and format of the report.

Covers

Chapter Twelve

Introducing the Report Designer

For more details about the Report Designer simply press F1.

When you first install Sage Line 50, you can immediately generate and print all of the reports and stationery to suit most business needs. If you use stationery supplied by Sage, the data should fit in the pre-printed stationery forms without adjustment.

There will be occasions though when you need a new report not already supplied, or you need to modify an existing one to suit your specific needs. The Report Designer lets you do all of this to meet any specific requirements that you have.

The Report Designer, although an integral part of Sage Line 50, is actually a complete windows application on its own. The Designer has its own Title Bar, Menu Bar, and Desktop area on which you can open multiple document windows. Each document window can hold an entirely separate layout file, which means you can work on several layouts at once, if you wish. To run the Report Designer do the following:

1   From the Line 50 menu bar select Tools, then Report Designer

2   The Report Designer window appears

Use the Report Designer to create or modify your own reports, stationery layouts, letters and labels.

3   Click here on each folder to see a list of existing layouts

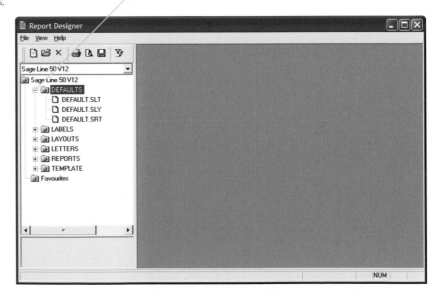

Creating a New Report

The following example shows you how to create a Customer Balance and Credit List for a single customer or a range of customers using the Report Wizard. The report contains the Customer's account reference, company name and account balance, together with their credit limit. The report is sorted to show the customer with the lowest balance first. The report also displays a balance total.

When the Wizard is finished the Report Designer appears with the new report or layout open ready for you to work on or preview.

To save time you can simply double-click the required variable to copy it to the Report Variables view.

For information about the various variables, simply click the Variable Info button. You can then print out the variable list for later reference.

Use the Favourites option to access the most frequently used reports.

1 Select Tools, then Report Designer from the Line 50 menu bar

2 Click File, New from the Report Designer menu, then click Next

3 Select Customer option

4 Enter report Title here

5 Click Next to continue

6 Select variable required from this list

7 Click Add button to copy to Report Variables view

8 Repeat Step 7 for all required variables

9 Click Next and Next again

10 Click Next again as grouping not required

11 Select SALES_LEDGER.BALANCE

12 Click the Add button

13 Click Next

Only numeric variables will be listed to total on when designing your report.

14 Select SALES_LEDGER.CREDIT_LIMIT

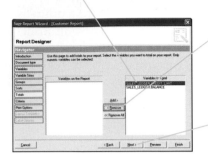

15 This total is not required, so click Remove to remove it from the list

16 Click Next

Criteria Status can be set to Disabled, Enabled or Preset. This controls the Criteria screen that appears prior to running the report.

17 Set Status to Enabled for Customer Ref and Tran Date

18 Click Next

19 Make any necessary changes to the printing options, i.e. Paper size or report Orientation

20 Click Finish to generate the report layout

Should you ever need to remove all the Total Variables simply click the << Remove All button.

The Report Designer now generates the appropriate report layout for you. You will be able to see how the layout is divided into sections, i.e. Page Header, Details, Page Footer, etc.

If the layout is not as required, you can modify the report later. First you need to check that it provides the information you require by running a report preview.

Always maximise your report layout window to view all the variables.

Previewing your Report

To speed up report design you can cut and paste groups of variables between two similar reports.

1 Click Preview to run your new report

2 The Criteria box appears

3 Enter Criteria details

4 Click OK to run the report

Be careful not to overwrite any existing reports. They may be useful to you later.

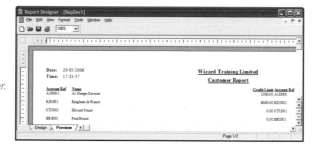

6 To close, click on File and Exit

5 To save, select Save As from File menu, enter a filename and click OK

Modifying an Existing Report

The Report Designer lets you modify existing report layout files and default reports supplied with the program. These will, however, need saving under a new filename.

As an example, you can modify the report just created and saved to include only those customers having a balance greater than £1000. This is called a filter, which is embedded in the report layout. To make these changes it is easier to start from the Sage Line 50 Customers option:

To remove your company's name and address from all your layout files, select Company Preferences from the Settings menu on the Sage Line 50 toolbar. Click on the Parameters tab and deselect the Print Address on Stationery check box, then click OK.

1 From the Customer toolbar click on the Reports option

2 Open correct folder, select your report and click Edit

3 Click Format, Filter

You can edit some Fixed Reports and save them to a new filename. The original report remains unchanged and your new report is added to the list.

4 In the Filter box click Build

If you make a mistake designing the report, select immediately the Edit Undo option from the Edit menu.

7 Click OK, Preview & Save

5 Select Sales_Ledger.Credit_Limit and click Add

6 Click > and type 1000 here, then OK

Opening Balances

This chapter explains how to enter opening balances for your customer, supplier, nominal and bank accounts as well as your products.

Covers

Chapter Thirteen

Introduction

Print off a copy of the Opening Balances checklist from the F1 Help system to guide you during set up.

It is important to set up opening balances correctly and in the right order. All accounts remain at zero until you enter opening balances for your Customers, Suppliers, Nominal, Bank and Products.

Where opening balances are carried forward, accurate figures need to be entered to reflect the true financial position of the business, for example, its Debtors, Creditors, Nominal Ledger Trial Balance, as well as its Stock.

Standard VAT and VAT Cash Accounting

Standard VAT calculates the VAT return on the invoices/credits you have raised for your customers or received from your suppliers, and any bank/cash payments or receipts or journal entries with vatable tax codes.

Posted Opening Balances for your customers and suppliers are displayed in the Trial Balance Report, which needs clearing before entering any Opening Balances for the nominal ledger accounts, bank accounts and products.

Customer opening balances can be entered as lump sum balances. It is recommended, however, that each outstanding invoice and credit note should be entered separately for cross referencing. Recording separate transactions will also provide accurate aged debtors analysis.

The second method, the VAT Cash Accounting scheme, is where the VAT return is calculated on the invoices/credits which you have received payment for from your customers or you have paid to your suppliers. It also includes any bank/cash payments or receipts or journal entries with vatable tax codes.

With VAT Cash Accounting each invoice and credit note must be entered for your customers individually, with the correct tax code.

Note that these are the Nominal Codes used in the Trial Balance:

1100 = *Debtors Control Account*

2100 = *Creditors Control Account*

9998 = *Suspense Account*

The same Standard VAT and VAT Cash Accounting conditions apply for entering opening balances for suppliers. Again, it is recommended for Standard VAT that separate transactions be recorded for outstanding invoices and credit notes to match up with payments later instead of grouping them all together in one opening balance. Separate transactions will again provide accurate aged creditors information.

Opening Balances – Standard VAT

Simply follow the same procedures as for Customers when entering opening balances for your Suppliers.

With the Standard VAT accounting method opening balances can be entered as a lump sum or individual transactions. You set up your customer balances using the Customer Record, accessed by using the Customers button on the Sage Line 50 toolbar.

Where customer information exists already, you can refer to the Aged Debtors Analysis and Detailed Customer Activity reports for cross referencing purposes and for checking that opening balances are recorded accurately. The Aged Creditors and Detailed Supplier Activity reports are also available for your suppliers.

To enter customer Opening Balance details

Simply follow the same procedures as for Customers when entering opening balances for your Suppliers.

1 From the Customers window click on the required record, then click Record on the toolbar

An Opening Balance can be entered as one total amount if a detailed breakdown is not required.

2 Click here to set up the Opening Balance

3 Enter invoice/credit note number

4 Enter original transaction date or last date of previous financial year

T9 is set as the default non-vatable tax code.

5 Enter Type

6 Enter Gross amount

7 Click Save to record details or Cancel to discard

Opening Balances – VAT Cash Accounting

Using this particular scheme each customer invoice and credit note needs entering individually with the correct tax code because VAT is only considered when payment is being made. The opening balances can be entered via the Batch Invoices or Credits screens.

To enter customer Opening Balance details

To identify reference numbers use the Audit Trail from within Financials.

1. From the Customers window click on the required record, then click Record on the toolbar

2. Click here to set up the Opening Balance

Enter the original date of invoice or credit note for accurate aged debtors analysis or last date of the previous financial year.

3. Enter invoice/credit note number

4. Enter original transaction date or last date of previous financial year

5. Enter Type

The default tax code and VAT appear automatically, but can be changed as necessary.

6. Enter Net amount. If you want to enter a single opening balance for this customer, enter total net amount of all invoices here

7. Tax Code and VAT are entered for you. Change if necessary then click Save to record details or Cancel to discard

Clearing Opening Balances From Trial Balance

Remember to always print a copy of your Trial Balance Report BEFORE clearing the opening balances.

When opening balances for your customers and suppliers are saved, they are posted to the Trial Balance. These entries need clearing or they will be duplicated when posting opening balances for your nominal ledger accounts. This will produce an incorrect Balance Sheet.

Before you start, make a note from your Trial Balance of the values of your Debtors and Creditors Control Accounts, your Sales Tax and Purchase Tax Control Accounts and your Suspense Account and whether each one is a debit or a credit, for example:

Trial Balance

When entering journal entries into the transaction table, use opposite values from the Trial Balance, i.e. Debit (+) and Credit (-).

Name	TC	Debit	Credit
Debtors Control Account	T9	30,687.19	
Creditors Control Account	T9		21,189.78
Suspense	T9		9,497.41
BALANCE		30,687.19	30,687.19

Once the relevant details have been noted, a Journal Entry from the Nominal Ledger needs to be made to clear the balances. Using the details from the above example, the entry would be as follows:

Journal Entry

The journal entry can only be saved when the value in the Balance box is zero.

Name	TC	Debit	Credit
Debtors Control Account	T9		30,687.19
Creditors Control Account	T9	21,189.78	
Suspense	T9	9,497.41	
BALANCE		30,687.19	30,687.19

Once you have noted what entries you need to make, you can add them to the Journal. When you process these entries, the opening balances in the Trial Balance will be cleared. To make the entries do the following:

1 From the Line 50 menu bar click Modules, then Nominal Ledger

2 Click on Journals from the Nominal Ledger window to bring up the Journals window

Always bear in mind that for a journal entry, the VAT is neither calculated nor posted for you to the VAT control account record.

3 The Ref. entry is optional. Type a reference if desired

4 Check for correct Date

N/C	Name	Dept	Details	T/C	Debit	Credit
1100	Debtors Control Account	0	Clear O/B	T9	0.00	30687.19
2100	Creditors Control Account	0	Clear O/B	T9	21189.78	0.00
9998	Suspense Account	0	Clear O/B	T9	9497.41	0.00
		0			0.00	0.00

Reference: CLEAROB Date: 28/05/2006 Balance: 0.00

30687.19 30687.19

Save Discard Memorise Recall Print List Close

If you make a mistake simply click on the Discard button and start again.

5 Enter details for both the credit and debits

6 Note, the default Tax code of T9 is entered for you by Sage Line 50

7 Check total Debit and Credit are equal and a zero balance is displayed in the Balance box

8 Click Save to process your journal or Discard to cancel

9 Click Close to return to Nominal Ledger window

Entering Balances Part Way Through the Year

When you use Sage Line 50 for the first time and you set up Product records, this is also a good time to have a stock take so that you know the details you are entering are accurate. Sage Line 50 can only produce accurate reports if the information you enter is correct. This is also a good time to check that Customer and Supplier details are still up-to-date.

Sage Line 50 needs Opening Balances in order to produce accurate financial statements. Since all accounts in all the ledgers have a zero balance when the program is first installed, it is important that the Opening Balances are entered as soon as possible. Without them your financial statements will not be accurate.

It is, however, quite possible to start using Sage Line 50 at any time through your financial year, and then enter the Opening Balances as they become available. For instance, if you have been in business for some time you will already have stock, products, customers and suppliers. You will have a transaction history. When you first start to use Sage Line 50 you will set up Records for your Customers, Suppliers, Products etc. This is when you can start to enter some Opening Balances.

If you do start to use Sage Line 50 part way through your financial year, you should contact your accountant as soon as possible for a detailed list showing all your outstanding Debtors and Creditors. You can then use this as the Opening Balances for your Customers and Suppliers.

You also need to ask for a Trial Balance from your accountant, which will give you the Opening Balances for each Nominal Ledger and Bank account.

If you do not enter a Cost Price in the Opening Product Setup box, then the product code is recorded as zero. This could affect your finance reports later.

You must at all times make sure that the information you enter is accurate. If you need to enter Opening Balances part way through your financial year, you will probably have a lot of Nominal Ledger opening balances to enter as well! It is important, therefore, that you enter these accurately otherwise your balance sheet will be incorrect.

You will also need to enter any year-to-date values from your Profit and Loss accounts. Your accountant should be able to provide you with this.

Nominal Ledger and Bank Account

When entering opening balances for your Nominal Ledger or Bank account, double-entry postings are applied by Sage Line 50. For example, if you post a debit opening balance of £100 to your Building Society account (1220 by default), Sage Line 50 automatically posts £100 as a credit to your Suspense Account (9998 by default).

After you have entered all your Nominal Ledger and Bank account opening balances, the balance of the Suspense Account should be zero again. A new Trial Balance needs to be printed to check that opening balances have been included for all your nominal accounts. If you still have a balance in your Suspense Account (i.e. it is not zero), an opening balance may have been omitted or a debit or credit misposted.

Nominal ledger opening balances

If you have money in the bank or building society, their statement shows you have a balance under the credit column. They owe you that money, you are the creditor. When this money is recorded in your accounts, such asset balances are recorded the opposite way round as debits. If you have money in your bank or building society, the balance must be entered as a debit.

1 From the Line 50 menu bar click Modules, then Nominal Ledger

2 Click on the required account   3 Click on the Record button

Enter an opening balance for each nominal account code that appears on your Trial Balance.

4 Click the O/B button to enter the balance

5 Enter opening balance details here

6 Click Save, then Close

Bank Opening Balances

You can also set up a Bank account Opening Balance directly from the Bank Record. To do this follow these steps:

An asset should always have a debit entry, whilst a liability should always have a credit entry.

1 From the Line 50 menu bar click Modules, then Bank

2 Click on the Bank Record you wish to set up an Opening Balance for and click on Record

3 Click the O/B button to bring up the Opening Balance Setup box

If you have money in your bank account, i.e. a debit, enter it as a Receipt. If you are overdrawn, i.e. a credit, enter it as a Payment.

4 Enter Date if different from default date

5 Enter opening balance as a Receipt or Payment. If you have money in your bank, this will be a Receipt

6 Click Save to record the Opening balance information

Opening Balances for Products

When you create a Product Record, you will probably enter an Opening Balance for that product if you already have some in stock. However, there will be times when you need to enter an Opening Balance at a later date to that when the Record was first set up.

If you do the latter, when you save the Opening Balance for a product, Sage Line 50 posts an Adjustment In transaction, which appears on the product reports. The valuation report will show the opening stock quantity at the cost price entered. To set up a Product Opening Balance:

1 From the Line 50 menu bar click Modules, then Products

2 Select the Product or products requiring an opening balance

3 Click Record

4 Click O/B button on the In Stock box

5 Enter Opening Balance details here

6 Click Save to return to the Products Record, then Close

Data Management

This chapter shows you important routines and procedures you need to regularly use for taking care of your data. Often data entered into the system is lost or corrupted by not following simple file maintenance. Backing up of data is essential to any business as problems often occur at the most inconvenient and crucial times.

Covers

Chapter Fourteen

Backing Up Data

Regular data backup (at least once daily) is essential in case of system error, when valuable data can be corrupted and sometimes lost. If this happens, you can at least restore important data files, reports and/or layout templates from your most up-to-date backup. A backup routine is provided by Sage Line 50 to automatically backup to your computer's Floppy Drive A, but this can be changed to save to any drive and/or directory you require.

Always keep your backups in a safe, secure place.

Backing up procedures vary from business to business; some use five disks for Monday to Friday and repeat their usage the following week. The important thing is to backup your data at least once a day! Sage Line 50 always prompts you to back up when you Exit the program, but to perform a backup at any other time, do the following:

1 From the Sage Line 50 menu, click on File

2 Click on Backup

3 Click No, unless you first want to check your data

Whilst Sage Line 50 gives you the option of checking your data before doing a backup,
it is advisable to click No and take the backup first, just in case errors are detected and you need copies of the data. Then take a final backup after the data check procedure, if required.

4 To backup to Sage Line 50's default drive, click OK; else, to make changes, follow Steps 5–6

5 Select required drive, directory and File Types to Backup

6 Click OK, then OK again

Restoring Data

It is always advisable to run the Check Data option from File, Maintenance after you have restored your data.

Hopefully you should never have to restore your files, but should you be unlucky and suffer data loss or corruption, the Restore procedure allows you to revert to a previous backup. The backup you use to restore data is up to you, but it will normally be the most recent.

The Restore facility allows data from your backup disks to replace your old data by erasing it and starting again. It is, therefore, very important to correctly label disks when you take a backup, and always keep them in a safe place. You may even consider keeping a second copy somewhere other than on the premises in case of fire or theft!

Restoring data will erase the current Sage Line 50 data and replace it with data from your backup disks.

Since the restore procedure erases your old data, any data you entered after the last backup is lost and will need to be entered again, so ensure you take frequent backups. Make sure that the Restore is first necessary, then do the following:

1 From the Sage Line 50 menu, click on File

2 Click on Restore

3 Click OK to restore data files from default drive, else go to Step 4

If you cancel whilst performing a Restore, Sage requires you to log in again.

4 If you are restoring from a different drive, select location here

5 Click OK to perform the restore

Changing Global Values

Use the Global Changes option to alter the values for either all or for a selected group of accounts or products.

Certain values in Sage Line 50, such as Credit Limits, have applications throughout the program. From time to time certain record values may need changing for all your records or for a selected group. To save time, these values can be changed quickly and easily by using the Global Changes Wizard. The Wizard guides you with on-screen instructions to make the necessary changes where required.

Values within the customer, supplier and nominal ledger records can be changed as well as certain values within your product records, for example the product sales price could be increased globally by 5% or the re-order level increased for a range of products. To run the Wizard:

Click on the Back button at any time to check whatever you entered in the previous screen or Cancel to abandon your changes.

1 From the Sage Line 50 menu, select Tools

2 Click on Global Changes to start the Wizard, then click Next to continue

3 Select the area where you want to make a Global Change

4 Click Next to continue

Remember that you can also use the Global Changes Wizard to quickly set up customer turnover and credit limits, supplier turnover and credit limits, and nominal budgets.

5 Select items to apply change to

6 Click Next to continue

To exit from a wizard at any point, choose the Cancel button or press ALT + F4.

7 Select type of change required and enter a value here before progressing

8 Click Next to continue

9 Check correct items are to be processed

Also use the Global Changes Wizard to quickly set up product sales and purchase prices, Discount Rates, Re-order Levels and Re-order Quantities for your Products.

10 Click Next to continue

11 Check that the details are correct. If you need to make any changes, use the Back button until you get to the appropriate screen, make the changes, then keep clicking Next to get back to this screen

Always check you have entered the correct information as you may not be able to easily undo changes.

12 Click Finish to action the changes

Whilst the Global Changes Wizard allows you to make changes quickly and easily, be very careful when using it and always double-check your values because when you click Finish, the changes you have entered are immediately actioned. In some cases these are quite major changes, such as increasing all product sales prices by a stated percentage. If you were to accidentally enter the wrong percentage, you cannot easily undo the resulting changes!

Importing Data

It can be very laborious entering a lot of data into certain records so Sage Line 50 lets you import data into the following record types – customers, suppliers, products and nominal ledger – provided, of course, it conforms to the correct file format. A group of new records can be created and imported directly into Line 50 or existing records updated with new details, replacing records being entered individually.

Avoid import errors by not exceeding maximum data unit length and using the correct data type, e.g. do not enter a decimal number into a integer data unit.

The text can be easily produced using any program which allows you to save the file in text format (.txt), for example, a word processing, spreadsheet or accounts package. The text must be in a specific format otherwise it will not be imported correctly and errors will be reported. These files are called CSV files (Comma Separated Values).

The following rules apply:

- A comma separates each unit of data, i.e. B01,Bolt,100,0.2

- Each data record takes up a single line.

- Each data record is terminated by pressing ENTER.

- Any spaces at the start or end of a data unit are ignored, but spaces within data units are included.

- Use quotes to include commas within a data unit, i.e. "25, Bell Lane".

- Each data unit in a record must be entered in strict order to avoid being imported incorrectly.

When importing account code data of customers and suppliers records, it is converted to upper-case and restricted to eight characters. Blank spaces are removed.

- Two consecutive commas (,,) forces a move to the next data unit.

An example of three typical CSV data records:

1,SI,BROWN,4000,2,Supplies,03/10/02,,27.15,T1,Y

2,SC,WHITE,4000,2,Credit,14/10/02,,35.00,T1,N

3,PI,BLACK,5000,4,Equipment,25/11/02,,52.50,T1,Y

To Import a Data File

A SPACE between two commas (, ,) causes the existing data to be erased.

1 From the Sage Line 50 menu, select File

2 Click Import

3 Click on correct Import Type here

Importing a blank unit of data does not overwrite existing data – it simply leaves it intact and forces a move to the next data unit. Use this feature for changing only selected data in a record.

4 Click Run to continue

5 Select Drive or Directory to Import from

A list of file import details is available from the help facility for customer/supplier records, nominal ledger audit trail transactions, stock records and stock transactions.

6 Enter Name of File to Import or select from list

7 Click Open

File Maintenance

Sage Line 50 provides five important options to manage and check the validity of your data files. These features include checking for input errors, allowing manual data error corrections, data compression, re-indexing and building new data files.

The Check Data option should be used on a daily basis to check for errors, so they can be quickly detected and rectified.

Error Checking

You should use the Check Data facility to check the validity of your data files. If necessary you can then make corrections where required. This facility needs to be run regularly, when making backups and after restoring data.

If there are problems whilst checking the data, a File Maintenance Problem Report dialog box appears which includes a Summary and details of Comments, Errors or Warnings.

1 From the Sage Line 50 menu, select File

2 Click on Maintenance

3 From the File maintenance window click Check Data

4 Checking Data Files box shows the progress

To print out an error report, select the category tab required from the File Maintenance Problems Report dialog box and click the Print button.

5 Check out details using Tabs

6 Click Fix to correct errors, else Close

Correcting Transactions

Any mistakes made while entering transactions can be corrected using the Corrections option from the File Maintenance window. These transactions, however, can only be edited or deleted if they are still held in the Audit Trail. To correct a transaction:

Use the Edit button to amend any reference for payments or receipts made against a transaction.

1 Click Corrections from the File Maintenance window

2 Select transaction to correct

Use the Find button to search for transactions.

3 Click Edit, then Yes to prompt

4 For changes to the customer/supplier account, details, reference or date, make your corrections here

5 For more changes click Edit

Journal entries cannot be amended using the Edit button. To do so you must select the Journals option from the Nominal Ledger toolbar and make the necessary adjustment by posting a journal entry with the opposite values.

6 To change the nominal account, details, department, amount or VAT amount/code, make your corrections here

7 Close and Save

If an amendment cannot be posted, a warning will appear detailing why not.

Reversing VAT Reconciled Transactions

You can delete a transaction provided it has not already been reconciled on the VAT Return. However, any VAT reconciled transaction will display a Reverse button instead of the Delete button in the Transaction Record window. To reverse VAT reconciliation on a transaction:

1 From the Posting Error Corrections window, select transaction and click Edit

2 To reverse VAT reconciliation click on the Reverse button

Take care when using the Rebuild option as it will clear the contents of your existing data files. USE WITH CAUTION.

3 Click Yes to confirm

Data Compression

When there has been a lot of activity, such as deletion or amendments of any records, use the Compress Data option to produce a new set of data files. Sage Line 50 will then reduce file size by removing these deleted records, freeing up disk space. To perform data compression, do this:

1 Click Compress Data from the File Maintenance Box

2 Click Compress

Use the ReIndex button to create new indexes for your ledger files should the Check Data option report errors.

3 Click Close

[ReIndex]

Rebuild

This Sage Line 50 option is for creating a new or selected set of data files. From the File Maintenance window:

1 Click Rebuild to run option

2 Select files to rebuild and click OK

Write Off, Refund and Return

Use these options to carry out accounting procedures that affect your customer and supplier accounts, e.g. cheque returns, invoice refunds and outstanding invoice transactions. The way you record these depends on your VAT method.

Sage Line 50 procedures for these functions vary depending on whether you are using the Standard VAT Scheme or VAT Cash Accounting.

Refunds

Use this facility for credit notes, payments on account and invoices where a money refund is required rather than a replacement of goods or provision of services. If you are using the Standard VAT Scheme, do the following:

From the Suppliers Tasks list select Write Off/Refund

For VAT Cash Accounting the transaction needs writing off manually. For more information, refer to Recording Refunds (VAT Cash Accounting) section of the Sage Line 50 Help.

2 Select where you want to make the amendments

3 Click Next

To find out if you are able to reclaim VAT paid on a Write Off, contact HM Revenue and Customs.

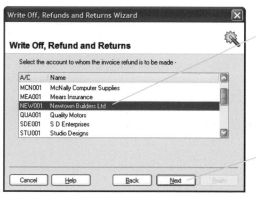

4 Select the account to whom the invoice refund is to be made

5 Click Next to Continue

…cont'd

Remember that this option is NOT suitable for anyone using VAT Cash Accounting as it does not adjust the VAT value for you.

6 Select the invoice being refunded

7 Click Next to continue

8 Select the bank account you wish to post the journal to

9 Click Next

10 Enter the correct date to use for the transaction here

11 Click Next

If the presented summary of information is incorrect, use the Back button to return to the appropriate box and modify.

12 The information you have entered is shown in this summary

13 Check carefully that it is all correct. Use the Back button if you need to make any change, else go to Step 14

14 Click Finish to post the transaction to your ledgers

Write Off

Using a credit note to refund an outstanding customer invoice is known as allocating the credit note to the customer invoice.

At times a customer will not or cannot pay an outstanding debt, so the amount can be written off to a bad debt account. The steps are very similar to a Refund, but fewer. Just select the appropriate Write Off for Step 2 (page 165) and follow the simple instructions.

Cheque Returns

Occasionally, you may need to record a cheque from a customer that you wish to cancel or that the bank has returned. If you use the Standard VAT Scheme, do this:

When a sales credit note is posted to the customer's account it assumes the same reference as the refunded invoice.

1. From the Customers Tasks list select Write Off/Refund

4. Click Customer Cheque Returns and Next

To record a refund using the Write Off, Refunds and Returns Wizard, the refund must need to be fully refunded and must not have been removed from the Audit Trail. If it has been removed or you need to make a partial refund, you must use the manual refund method.

5. Select account, click Next

6. Select the cheque and carry out Steps 9–14 on Page 166

Posting Contra Entries

Where you have a customer who is also one of your suppliers, you may offset sales invoices against your supplier's purchase invoices. To do this, you use the Contra Entries option from the Tools menu to match one or more sales invoices with your purchase invoices. Sage Line 50 will then automatically update the appropriate ledgers. To post a Contra Entry:

If VAT Cash Accounting is being used, make sure the selected transactions have matching tax codes.

1 From the Sage Line 50 menu, click Tools

2 Click on Contra Entries to bring up the Contra Entries window

You cannot amend any of the values shown in the Total boxes.

3 Select Customer (Sales Ledger) and Supplier (Purchase Ledger) accounts

If your totals do not match, a warning message appears asking whether you want to make part-Contra Entries for the lowest amount. If acceptable click the Yes button or No to cancel the Contra Entries.

4 Select outstanding invoice (on sales side) from the list

5 Select invoice to apply Contra Entry for

6 Click OK to finish

Run Period End Functions

Period End options are essential monthly and year end procedures for updating the accounting system. For example, for posting accruals, prepayments and depreciation. The Audit Trail can then be cleared of any unwanted transactions whilst stock can be cleared from your Product history if you so wish.

Through running these procedures, you will also be preparing Sage Line 50 so that you are ready to enter transactions for the new financial period.

Month End

At each month end it is important to post your prepayments, accruals and depreciation values. Sage Line 50 will process these transactions automatically and update your nominal account records and Audit Trail for you. The option also exists to clear down your month to date turnover figures for your customer and supplier records.

Once you have run the Month End procedures, this is an opportune time to produce some of your financial reports, for example, the Profit and Loss, Balance Sheet, Trial Balance, Budget and Prior Year Analysis reports. Customer statements and Aged analysis reports for Debtors and Creditors will also prove useful.

Month End Guidelines

Here is a check list for the Month End:

1   Check all relevant transactions have been posted.

2   Check recurring entries have been set up and processed.

3   Check prepayments, accruals and depreciation have been set up.

4   Complete your bank reconciliation.

5   Print product history, valuation and profit reports.

6   Post product journals for your Profit and Loss & Balance Sheet.

If program date needs changing for Month End procedure, select Change Program Date from the Settings menu. Remember to re-set the date back to the correct date.

Always Backup your data files before and after running Month End procedures.

Use File Maintenance Check and Compress Data options to check your files.

After following the Month End guidelines it is time to run the month end procedure. You will probably want to run it on a day other than the actual last calendar day of the month, as this is often more convenient. You will therefore have to change the program date first. To do this, simply follow these steps:

The month end routine is necessary if you have Prepayments, Accruals, Depreciation, or you wish to clear down the turnover figures for Customers and Suppliers.

1 First back up your data files

2 From the Sage Line 50 menu bar click Settings

Always print off your month end reports for future reference.

4 Enter the last day of the month here

3 Click on Change Program Date

5 Click OK

The Year End is an ideal time to remove any fully paid transactions or unwanted records, leaving only outstanding items on your ledgers at the start of the new Financial Year.

6 From the Sage Line 50 menu, click on Tools

7 Select Period End

If you have multicompany Sage Line 50, you can use the Consolidation option from Period End to merge the data from your separate companies to form one set of financial accounts.

8 Click on Month End

9 Tick the required options

10 Click OK to run the Month End procedure

Year End

Before you run the Year End, Month End procedures must be completed, together with any final adjustments.

Take at least two backups of your data files both before and after running the Year End routine.

First, when you run Month End on the last month of the current financial year, DO NOT clear the Audit Trail. Once values for the month end have been checked and you are satisfied that they are correct, set the program date to the last date of the current financial year and run Year End:

1 Set the program date to the last day of the financial year by doing Steps 1–5 on Page 170

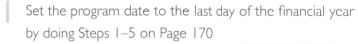

2 From the Sage Line 50 menu, click on Tools

After Year End check your Financial Year Start Date is correct before entering new transactions.

3 Select Period End

4 Click on Year End

5 Tick here to update your budget figures for each nominal ledger profit and loss account and each product record with the actual values from the year just ending

You must not consolidate companies that have different base currencies.

6 Change Year End Journals Date if necessary

7 Select Output

8 Click OK to run

Lastly, remove any unwanted Customer, Supplier, Nominal, Bank and Product records and reset system date. You are now ready to continue entering transactions for the new financial year.

Clearing the Audit Trail and Stock

This option lets you remove paid and reconciled transactions prior to a specified date from the Audit Trail. This makes the ledgers easier to read. Reconciled transactions on the nominal ledger are brought forward as opening balances.

Only paid, allocated and reconciled transactions are removed from the Audit Trail.

Sage Line 50 can store up to 2,000,000,000 transactions in the Audit Trail, so transactions do not have to be removed, but by deleting unwanted transactions, it will free disk space and provide faster access to information.

Before running the Clear Stock option, you should back up your data and print your stock valuation and stock history reports. Do likewise before clearing the Audit Trail.

From the Tools menu, select Period End, click Clear Audit Trail, then Next on the first two prompt screens

2 Enter required date

3 Click Next, then Process to clear the Audit Trail

Clear Stock

This option can be run as part of the Month End and Year End procedures. It allows you to decide when to clear transactions from your Product History.

From the Tools menu, select Period End and click Clear Stock

Departmental reporting and activity will be affected by removing transactions from the Audit Trail.

2 Click Yes to continue

3 Enter date here

4 Click OK

The Task Manager

This chapter shows you how to use the Task Manager for setting up useful functions such as a reminder list of tasks to do, i.e. bills to pay, people to contact, etc. It also lets you quickly view the status of your accounts, invoices, sales orders and purchase orders as well as check how much you owe and vice versa.

Covers

Chapter Fifteen

Features of the Tasks Option

Use the Tasks option to set up a list of jobs that you need to do and to prompt you of any tasks that are currently due, overdue or recently completed. By setting up these tasks it acts as a reminder of the actions you need to take to run your business efficiently, produces important information and saves valuable time.

Use the Contacts option to check the people you need to speak to, or have spoken with recently, plus any overdue calls that need to be made. This information is linked directly to the customer and supplier record Contacts tab and will update the relevant future, today, overdue and completed contacts folder.

You can use the Tasks option to help you:

- Set up a list of tasks that you need to do and also view any tasks that are either completed, due or overdue

- List people you need to contact today or in the future, or record and view any contacts that you have 'completed' or that are 'overdue'

- Record the bills you receive and view bills that are paid, due for payment or overdue

- Check how much you owe your suppliers and, more important, find out how much you are owed by your customers

- Check the account status of your customers and suppliers. For example, you will be able to see at a glance which accounts are over the credit limit, inactive or on-hold

- View and keep track of any recurring entries you have set up in Sage Line 50

If you need to clear all your To Do entries in one go simply click on Clear To Do Entries from the Settings menu.

- Quickly check the status of invoices, sales orders and purchase orders. For example, you may want to see which invoices or credit notes are due for printing or which have yet to be posted

- Keep track of your stock levels. You can easily and quickly check for out of stock items, items which are below re-order level, on order or which have been allocated

The Task Manager Desktop

Your Sage Line 50 Task Manager desktop features a menu bar, a stacked toolbar, an application toolbar and a split screen, with tree view on the left and list view on the right.

From the desktop you can set up tasks, remind yourself of jobs to do etc. To bring up the desktop do the following:

The Application toolbar offers different options with different functions, depending upon the Tasks chosen from the Stacked toolbar.

1 From the Sage Line 50 menu, click on Tools, then click Task Manager

2 The Menu Bar provides a list of options using drop-down menus

3 The stacked toolbar area

4 List View area

Options available from the Application toolbar are also available from the Tasks menu. These include New, Open, Delete, Pay and Properties.

Use the List View screen (right hand side of the screen) as a shortcut to your tasks, transactions, bills, recurring entries etc. by simply double-clicking on the required entry.

5 Click on the Tasks or Company buttons for the respective toolbars

6 Select a folder in the Tree View area to bring up a list

7 Resize the View areas by dragging from here

Setting Up a To Do Task

Use the To Do option to create a list of tasks you need to complete. The type of tasks include a General Reminder, Send overdue letters, Print management reports, etc. Any additional information that may prove useful can be entered within the Description and Notes boxes.

Once saved, the task appears in the Current Tasks folder on the To Do list. This list can then be viewed at any time. To set up a To Do task, proceed as follows:

If the Task Complete box is selected, the task is moved from the Current Tasks or Overdue Tasks list to the Complete Tasks list.

When you save your task it appears in the Current Tasks folder on the To Do List.

To delete a task, simply highlight it from the Current, Overdue or Completed Tasks list and click the Delete button from the Task Manager Toolbar.

1 From the Task Manager, click on the To Do option from the Tasks stacked toolbar

2 Click New from the application toolbar

4 Enter date when task is due for completion

3 Select the reminder type from the drop down list box

5 Enter a suitable Description, e.g. chase overdue payments

7 Click OK to save

6 Type any special instructions here

8 Check here when complete

Recording a New Bill

The Bills option provides a useful and convenient way of recording all your bills, such as rates, rent, etc. Once the payment information is entered and saved, the bill will appear in the Current Bills folder on the Bills list. These details can be edited if required at this stage.

Use the Task Manager then to quickly view which bills are paid, due or overdue. To record a new bill:

When the bill details are saved, it will appear in the Current Bills folder on the Bills list. If required you can then edit your bill details.

1 Using Task Manager, click on the Bills option from the Tasks stacked toolbar

2 Click New from the File menu

3 Enter the nominal code for the bill to, e.g. if paying your telephone bill the default nominal ledger account is 7502

4 Describe your transaction here

References entered into the Ref box will appear in the Audit Trail for cross referencing.

If a bill is not paid by the Due Date, the task is moved to the Overdue Bills folder.

5 Enter Net amount of the bill here

7 Enter date bill is due to be paid

6 Enter date bill received

8 Check all details and click OK to save

Paying a Bill

Use the Pay option to quickly and easily pay any current or outstanding bills which have been previously set up using Task Manager. To action bill payment the only detail required is the Bank Account nominal code you want to pay the bill from, as shown here:

After paying a selected bill, it is moved from the Current Bills or Overdue Bills folder to the Paid Bills folder. The bill payment details are updated on the Bill Record.

1 Select Bills from the Tasks stacked toolbar

2 Select either Current Bills or Overdue Bills folder from the Tree view

3 Select the bill required from the List View

4 Click the Pay option from the application toolbar

An alternative way to pay a bill is by selecting the Pay option from the toolbar.

5 Enter nominal code of Bank account to pay the bill from

6 Click OK to pay the bill

7 The bill is now paid and moves into the Paid Bills folder

8 Click on the Paid Bills folder and double-click on the bill you have just paid

To print the activity on a certain nominal account just click Nominal, then Reports in Line 50 and select the Nominal Activity report layout.

9 Note the Bill Record is updated to show payment details

10 Click OK to close

Accounts Due

Use the Accounts Due option from the Tasks stack to identify who owes you money, i.e. Sales Overdue, Sales Due and Sales Within Settlement. You can also check who you owe money to by viewing the Purchases Overdue, Purchases Due and Purchases Within Settlement folders.

Use the Phone button to automatically dial your customer telephone number. Your computer (with modem) needs to share the same line as your telephone.

To find out which customers owe you money

1 From the Tasks stacked toolbar, select Accounts Due and click the Sales Overdue folder

2 Note transaction list of overdue payments

3 For more details, select a transaction

4 Click Properties from the application toolbar

To view details of different transactions on the list, click the First, Previous, Next or Last buttons.

Transaction Details

Account Details

A/C	STE002	Name	Steven Stephenson
No.	1387	Contact	Steven Young
		Telephone	0151 977 8876

Values

Net	2940.00
Tax	501.64
Paid	0.00
	3441.64

Transaction Details

| Type | Sales Invoice | Ref | 71 |
| Details | PC Combo Pack 6 | Date | 28/03/2006 |

First Previous Next Last   OK

5 The Transaction Details window appears

7 When finished click OK

For a printout of debtors refer to the Customers Reports window.

6 Use these buttons to move between different transactions in the list

Account Status

The Account Status option lets you view accounts that match certain criteria. For example, Sales Over Credit Limit, Sales On Hold, Purchase Over Credit Limit or Purchase On Hold. If you require more detailed information about a transaction, select it and click the Properties button from the application toolbar.

In the Account Details window use the First, Previous, Next and Last buttons to move between different account transactions.

1 From the Sage Line 50 Task Manager window, choose the Account Status option from the Tasks stacked toolbar

2 Select the folder you require from the Tree View list

3 Highlight the required account from the List view

4 Click the Properties button on the toolbar

You can print out a list of customers On Hold or customers Over Credit Limit from the Sage Line 50 Customers, Reports window.

5 When finished, click OK to exit

The Recurring Option

Using the Task Manager you can view any recurring entries you have set for various transaction types, namely Receipt, Payment, Journal Debit or Journal Credit.

You can view further details on the transactions, but you cannot change these details. To view details on a recurring payment you set up in Sage Line 50, do the following:

To set up your recurring entries simply select the Recurring option from the Bank toolbar. Refer to chapter 5, page 67, for more information about setting up recurring entries.

1 From the Sage Line 50 Task Manager window, choose the Recurring option from the Tasks stacked toolbar

2 Select the folder you require from the Tree View list, e.g. Payments

3 Highlight the required payment from the List view

4 Click the Properties button on the application toolbar

For detailed information about a recurring entry, select the transaction and choose the Properties option from the application toolbar.

5 The details appear for the selected recurring entry

Remember that you cannot change the recurring entry details from within the Task Manager.

6 Click Close when finished

Stock Option

The Task Manager is a handy way of keeping track of your stock. It provides you with a fast and efficient way of seeing what is out of stock, below the reorder level, on order and allocated.

By using Task Manager for regular monitoring of stock you can make decisions about items which need re-ordering or stock you are waiting for.

Stock transactions are for viewing only; a properties facility is not available within Task Manager.

Sage Line 50 can only provide accurate reporting and stock tracking if the correct information has been entered in the first place. Plan to make full use of Sage Line 50's extensive stock details recording facilities.

1 Select the Stock option from the Tasks stacked toolbar

3 Relevant details appear in the list area for your information

2 Select the folder required in the Tree View

4 Click here to scroll across all the details

Invoices Option

Within Task Manager you can view the status of any invoices or credit notes that you have recorded.

An alternative way to view your invoices is to select Tasks from the Task Manager menu bar and click Invoices.

Invoices and credit notes are listed separately depending on whether they have been printed or posted. You can also quickly view which invoices or credit notes need to be printed or posted.

For example, do the following to quickly view a list of invoices which you have not yet posted:

1 From the Task Manager window, click on the down button on the Tasks stacked toolbar until Invoices appears

2 Click on the Invoices option

3 Select Inv to Post folder

To print/post an invoice or credit note or record an invoice/credit note number, return to the Line 50 Invoicing option, then select your transaction and use the Print/Post option.

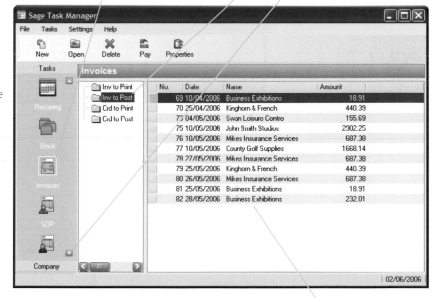

4 A list of invoices not yet printed appears

Sales Order Processing

From Task Manager you can view the status of your Sales Orders directly. A selection of folders is available for you to view the type of sales orders required. For example, orders that are 'To Allocate', 'Cancelled', 'Held', etc.

You can also access Sales Orders by selecting Tasks from the Task Manager menu and clicking on Sales Orders.

It is important to remember, however, that you can only view the details in this screen. If you need to create a new Sales Order or make any changes, you will have to return to the SOP option in Sage Line 50.

As an example, if you wanted a list of allocated Sales Orders not yet delivered, you could use the SOP Reports facility to print out a suitable report, or you can do a quick view from the Task Manager as follows:

1 From Task Manager, click the SOP option on the Tasks Stacked toolbar

2 Select the Allocated, to Despatch folder

You will need to return to the SOP option in the Sage Line 50 to perform any sales order functions.

3 A list of Completed Sales Orders appears in the View area

Purchase Order Processing

Just as with Sales Orders, use the Task Manager to quickly display the status of your Purchase Orders when you do not need a printed copy. Options available are To Order and To Deliver.

To access Purchase Orders from the Task Manager menu, select Tasks and click Purchase Orders.

For example, to view a list of Purchase Orders that are 'To Deliver' follow these simple steps:

1 From the Task Manager window, choose the POP option from the Tasks stacked toolbar (you may have to use the down button on the stacked toolbar to bring it into view)

2 Select the To Deliver folder in the Tree View

You cannot alter transaction details using this Task Manager facility. You will need to return to the POP option in Sage Line 50 to perform any purchase order functions.

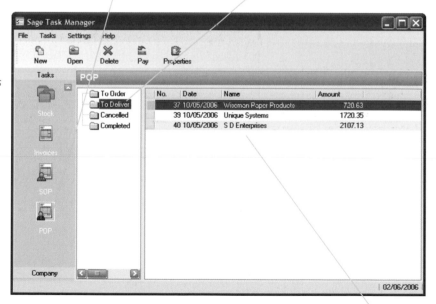

3 A list of Purchase Orders To Deliver appears in the View area

The Company Stack

This feature is useful for quickly viewing your Company Details, such as Name, Address, Telephone, Fax, VAT Reg. No., Web Site and E-mail.

You can also select Company Details from the Settings menu on the Sage Line 50 Task Manager toolbar to view or amend your Company Details.

These details, however, cannot be edited using this screen. To do so you will need to exit from the Task Manager and return to Sage Line 50 toolbar. Then, select Company Preferences from the Sage Line 50 Settings menu and make your changes using the Address tab (see page 11).

To quickly view Company Details from the Task Manager just do the following:

1 Click on the Company button at the foot of the stacked toolbar

2 Click on Company Details to view information

3 The Details window appears

4 Click OK to close

Index

A

B

C

O

P

Q

R

S